ELK!

PROVEN STRATEGIES FOR ELK HUNTING SUCCESS

SHADY OAK PRESS

MINNETONKA, MINNESOTA

About the Author

Bob Robb's articles and photographs have appeared regularly in most all the major outdoor magazines for nearly two decades. His big game hunting adventures have taken him around the world, including to Africa, Asia, Europe, South America, Canada and Mexico. Bob, an accomplished big game hunter with both firearms and bow, has made more than 50 elk hunts across the western states, Alaska and Canada and has hunted elk in Mongolia, where they are called Maral stags. An editor for several national hunting magazines for 15 years, Bob is now a full-time freelance writer. He lives in Arizona.

ELK!

Proven Strategies for Elk Hunting Success

Tom Carpenter
Creative Director

Jen Weaverling
Production Editor

Randy Hoepner
Cover Design

Heather Koshiol
Book Development Coordinator

Julie Cisler, Clarinda Color
Book Design and Production

David Rottinghaus
Color Illustrations

Phil Aarrestad
Commissioned Photography

1 2 3 4 5 6 / 12 11 10 09 08 07
ISBN 13: 978-1-58159-348-8

Distributed by:
Sterling Publishing Co., Inc.
387 Park Avenue South
New York, NY 10016-8810

For information about custom editions, special sales, premium and corporate purchases, please contact Sterling Special Sales Department at 800-805-5489 or specialsales@sterlingpub.com

PHOTO CREDITS

Donald M. Jones: cover, back cover, 1, 4, 5, 16 (bottom), 21 (bottom), 25, 37, 39, 48–49, 52, 58, 60, 64, 65, 78, 80, 81, 82, 86, 95 (top right), 95 (bottom left), 96, 98 (bottom right), 98 (bottom left), 99, 100, 101, 104, 105, 109, 112, 113, 114–115, 124–125, 127, 128, 129, 130, 132, 134, 137, 155 (both), 157; **Lance Krueger:** 11, 13 (bottom), 14, 18, 29, 32, 41, 42, 56–57, 59, 72–73, 75, 89, 94, 95 (bottom right), 95 (top left), 98 (center), 98 (top right), 106, 121, 154; **Lon E. Lauber:** 45, 74, 103; **Bill McRae:** 6–7, 17, 21 (top), 27, 33, 38, 43, 51, 54, 79, 83, 84, 90–91, 93, 95 (left center), 120, 146, 149, 150–151; **Bob Robb:** 47, 50, 138–139; **Leonard Rue Enterprises:** 12 (both), 13 (top), 61; **Ron Spomer:** 153 (bottom); **Tom Tietz:** 8–9, 10, 15, 16 (top), 19, 20, 70–71, 85, 87, 92, 102, 116, 117, 119, 140, 143, 152, 153 (top); **Jim Van Norman:** 156. **Remaining photographs property of NAMG:** 22–23, 24, 26, 28, 30, 31, 34, 36, 40, 44, 46, 53, 55, 62, 97, 126, 141, 144, 148.

SHADY OAK PRESS
12301 Whitewater Drive
Minnetonka, MN 55343

Table of Contents

Chapter Six

Chapter Seven

Chapter Eight

Chapter Nine

Chapter Ten

Foreword

Elk hunters come in many forms. Of course, those of us not fortunate enough to live in elk country have to plan extra hard, pack extra heavy and then travel extra long to get to where the elk are. But the result—time in some of the most beautiful places on earth, hunting one of North America's finest game animals—is worth it.

And then there are those lucky Westerners among us who have elk right in their own state. Of course, the hunting is still hard, but at least home is not so far away and maybe, if you don't get your elk the first week in camp, you can get out a time or two again to try and fill the tag.

And no matter who it is doing the hunting, there are different philosophies and commitments. There are far-gone mountain men who will bivouac at treeline in order to be in position on the edge of a good meadow at first light the next day, waiting for the bull of their dreams. Others are happy to sneak across a lowland sagebrush meadow and take a fine-eating cow on a snowy, late-season morning and call it good.

But no matter where you live or hunt, or how you go at it, elk are tough to outsmart. Make no bones about it—you will hunt long and hard to take a good bull elk fair-and-square. And the key to your success will be what you know about elk behavior, and how you use that to your advantage in the way you hunt.

That's where Bob Robb—author of *ELK!*—comes in. His philosophy on (and commitment to) elk hunting are about as simple as you can get: Know and love the animal; love the country; give them both everything you've got; and just get out there and hunt, hunt, hunt. No one knows elk better, hunts them harder or with more passion (with rifle, muzzleloader and bow), and can't wait for the next season even when he's still nursing this season's beat-to-a-pulp feet and recovering from lost sleep due to weeks' worth of 3:00 a.m. wake-up calls.

We know you love your elk … or will, if you're preparing for your first elk hunt. So we've brought you the best elk hunting book ever, from one of the most successful elk hunters alive today. Take heed of these *Proven Strategies for Elk Hunting Success*. Read, look, learn and enjoy. Then put all the knowledge to good use on your next elk hunting trip.

Good hunting, and good luck.

Tom

Tom Carpenter
Shady Oak Press

INTRODUCTION

Approaching the millennium, what passionate big-game hunter has not dreamed of stepping back to a simpler time, following the footsteps of Lewis and Clark as they explored the Rocky Mountain West? Of revisiting the days when undeveloped land stretched as far as the eye could see, when game was plentiful, when a person answered to no one but his own conscience?

Each year thousands of hunters do exactly that, heading into the high mountains or tackling the dense Pacific coastal rain forest jungles in pursuit of *Cervus elaphus nelsoni*, the Rocky Mountain elk, and its close cousin, *C. a. roosevelti*, the Roosevelt elk. Certainly the West has grown up, and there isn't the open space there was when Lewis and Clark first saw it. But each fall, on millions of acres of both public and private lands across the West—and, increasingly, areas east of the Mississippi River—hunters thrill to the sound of a bull elk's primal bugle, a glimpse of a patch of tan hide slipping through the thick timber, the glint of sunlight off a massive rack of antlers. They marvel at the majestic mountains, deep valleys and raging rivers that both define elk country and challenge our toughness—both mentally and physically—as no other region can.

I remember my first elk hunt as vividly as if it were yesterday. It was in the late 1970s, and I'd scrimped and saved enough money to take an outfitted horseback hunt into Idaho's rugged Selway Bitterroot Wilderness. Back then you could rifle hunt bugling bulls during the September rut, and I shot a big 6x6 that scored nearly 330 Boone and Crockett Club points. I was hooked deeply and was, at that time, naïve enough to think I could take a big bull every year. It was 10 years and over a dozen more tough, on-my-own elk hunts before I bettered that bull.

Since that first hunt, I've hunted elk several times in every Western state in which I can obtain a tag, as well as in Alaska, Canada and even Mongolia, where their Maral stag is a virtual clone of *C. a. nelsoni*. From the rain forests of the coast to the tall peaks of Colorado; from the grassy plains of northern New Mexico to the rugged mountains of British Columbia; from the sweltering days of early September bowhunts to the bitter, subzero cold of Thanksgiving near Yellowstone National Park, the memories run powerful and deep.

The future of elk—and of elk hunting—is bright. It's a door to the past and a path to the future. There is no big-game hunting adventure in all of North America that compares to hunting elk. Try it sometime, and you'll see what I mean.

—Bob Robb

Chapter 1

All about Elk

Many first-time elk hunters don't live anywhere near Western elk country. Most have never even seen an elk before they go forth on their first elk hunt. Obviously, they've never had a chance to learn firsthand what elk are, how they act and where and how they live.

For these folks, stepping off an airplane or out of their trucks and into the majestic elk mountains can be something of a shock. The country is so big, so imposing, so intimidating—the doubts begin to creep in. How the heck am I supposed to find an elk? Where in the world do I begin looking? How do I begin looking? In essence, these ill-prepared hunters have been defeated before they ever begin. They're a big reason that success rates for general elk seasons in all Western elk states are below 25 percent. Often, they are half that.

Even if you're a Westerner, the equation is still the same—you have to know elk, find them and then get up on them in order to have any chance for success.

And yet thousands of hunters—many of them nonresidents—have enjoyable, successful elk hunts every fall. These intrepid outdoorsmen and women have taken the time to learn about elk, researched their trips and given themselves enough time to make it happen.

It all begins with learning about elk—what they are, where and how they live, what they eat and how they react to different weather patterns and unwanted intrusions into their lives. Such knowledge not only increases your chances of finding and then harvesting elk, but also increases the overall enjoyment of your elk hunt. Armed with this knowledge, you'll soon find yourself becoming a part of the landscape, moving in harmony with the natural world into which you've ventured.

Want to learn more? Then read on ...

Elk: What Are They?

Few big-game animals inspire North American hunters like elk do. And rightly so. Elk, *Cervus elaphus*, are powerful animals with large bodies and even larger antlers. Their meat is some of the most delicious and nutritious in all of nature. Despite their gregarious nature, elk are secretive—especially when pressured by people. For many sportsmen and women, elk are the ultimate challenge.

Today there are more elk in North America than at any time since the turn of the 19th century. Yet their history remains something of a mystery. It is believed that North America was home to somewhere around 10 million elk prior to the arrival of the first European settlers. Sir Francis Drake is believed to have spotted elk off the California coast in 1579, calling what is believed to be a Tule elk "a very large and fat Deere." Settlers along the east coast saw elk too, which in those days lived in large numbers all across the continent. Written accounts document elk living from New England south through at least the Chesapeake Bay region.

By 1907, however, elk numbers had dwindled to less than 100,000 animals as the rapid expansion of Western colonization took its toll. In 1922,

Compare where elk originally roamed (inset) vs. now (main map). Courtesy Rocky Mountain Elk Foundation, 1-800-CALL ELK.

it is believed that a total of only 92,000 elk remained, of which a little more than 37,000 lived in Yellowstone National Park, the Teton National Forest and parts of Canada.

Estimates place the current elk population at a little more than one million animals ... and growing, thanks in no small measure to efforts by sport hunters. In fact, there are so many elk in some areas that local residents are calling for herd reductions as the powerful, voracious elk eat more than their share of hay and other crops. Elk may also contribute to the decline of other native game, notably mule deer.

During the glacial age, there were 10 subspecies of *Cervus* in North America. Of these, 6 are extinct. The 4 remaining subspecies include:

Rocky Mountain elk (*Cervus elaphus nelsoni*): Our most common elk, they can be found throughout the West, as well as in states to which they have been transplanted, including diverse areas like Pennsylvania, Michigan, Virginia, Oklahoma, Texas, Kansas and the Dakotas, as well as parts of eastern Canada. Mature bulls weigh somewhere around 700 pounds and cows 525 pounds, though this can vary widely depending on where they live.

Roosevelt elk (*C. e. roosevelti*): The largest-bodied elk are found in the rain forests of the

Rocky Mountain elk.

Roosevelt elk.

Pacific Northwest, from northern California up through Oregon and Washington, coastal British Columbia and Vancouver Island, and scattered islands in southeast Alaska as well as Afognak and Raspberry Islands, Alaska. Mature bulls weigh between 700 and 1100 pounds, although records show some Afognak bulls as having field dressed at nearly 1000 pounds. Cows weigh between 575 and 625 pounds.

Manitoba elk (*C. e. manitobensis*): The second-largest elk, Manitoba elk are located in isolated pockets of the southwestern corner of Manitoba, the southern half of Saskatchewan and southeastern Alberta. Mature bulls weigh in at about 800 pounds and cows at about 600 pounds.

Tule elk (*C. e. nannodes*): Our smallest elk, Tule elk live only in various locations throughout California. Numbering an estimated 500,000 before the mid-1800s, by the mid-19th century their population had dropped to exactly 8 animals. Today there are an estimated 3,100 Tule elk. Mature bulls weigh just 400 pounds, while cows average 325 pounds.

Elk are the second largest member of the North American deer family, surpassed only in body and antler size by moose *(Alces alces).*

Elk have no useful teeth in the front portion of their upper jaw, wearing instead a dental pad over their lower front teeth like other grazers. They have a total of 32 teeth including the "ivories" so prized by hunters. These are not real ivory, but instead incisiform canine teeth. Also known by the terms "whistlers," "buglers" and "elk teeth," these two teeth are located in the forward portion of the upper jaw.

Elk antlers are, of course, what serious elk hunters dream about. They are a fascinating part of the animal's physiology.

A mature Rocky Mountain bull elk's antlers usually consist of a single long main beam between 40 and 60 inches long that sweeps up and back from the head. These antlers are home to between two and six distinct tines, or points; non-typical points are possible as well. The first two tines, called the brow and bez tines, grow close together at the base of the skull, sweeping outward from the bull's face. The third, or trez, tine begins farther up the beam, usually angling forward. The "royal" or "sword" point, as the fourth point is commonly called, is generally the longest point of all and is usually the dominant feature of the entire rack. The fifth point grows off the main beam behind the royal point, forming a fork with the end of the main beam, which is always counted as a point as well. Most mature bulls grow no more than six points per

Tule elk.

Red stag.

side, though some old, large bulls never grow more than five points, and a rare few will grow seven, eight or even nine points. This antler conformation is typical of the Manitoba subspecies as well. The elk pictured below sports a classic rack, and you can clearly see each of the antler features described.

The only difference between the racks of the above two subspecies and the Roosevelt and Tule elk subspecies is the "crowning" at the end of the main beam on many Roosevelts and Tules. Here, instead of the simple fork found on the Rocky Mountain and Manitoba elk, the antlers will sometimes—but not always—form a "crown," or cluster, of small points akin to those found on the red stag of Europe and South America. A full set of antlers from a mature bull of any elk subspecies—except the smallish Tule elk—will weigh between 20 and 30 pounds.

Elk have played a prominent part in the history of North America. Natives used their flesh and fat for food, and their hides for shelter and clothing. Tools, toys and ceremonial ornaments were crafted from elk bones, antlers and teeth. In the modern West, elk continue to play a prominent role in shaping the future. Contemporary land management planning and decisions are rarely made today without considering the impact on wildlife, and elk are often in the center ring of these decisions.

A Year in the Life of an Elk

To become a successful big-game hunter, you must learn all you can about the animal you wish to pursue. It just makes sense that the more you know about your quarry, the better your chances of success. You need to know everything about it: what it eats and where it sleeps; how it is affected by weather, people and roads; and what it likes and dislikes. After all, you can't shoot an elk if you can't find one. With meager knowledge of the animal itself, instead of going elk hunting you'd be better served spending your money on lottery tickets—your chances of finding an elk will be that low.

The more you learn about elk, their habits and haunts, where they live during the various seasons, and what they do during "odd" periods—a freak early-season snowstorm or an unusual streak of warm weather late in the year—the better your chances at finding them become.

To get you started, here's a brief rundown of a year in the life of an elk.

Summer Magic

After being carried by the cow for 8 to 8½ months, elk calves are born in summer, usually early June, when the grasses are tall and lush, temperatures mild and water easily found. Single calves are common, twins a rarity. Calf elk weigh around 25 to 30 pounds at birth. Calving grounds are located in the upper reaches of the elk's winter range, where there are lots of grassy meadows bordered by dark escape-cover timber.

For the first 2 to 4 weeks after birth, cows and their newborn calves stay away from the herd while each mother tends to her calf just getting used to its legs. After that, the cows and calves herd up, with herds of cows, calves and young bulls often numbering in the hundreds. It is interesting to note that other cows will sometimes act as babysitters while a mother goes off to feed on her own for a short time.

Where are the bulls? Mature bulls keep to themselves during this time, congregating in small bachelor herds. Bulls begin antler growth anytime between January and June, depending on their age and testosterone level and the changing photoperiod (amount of daylight vs. darkness each day). The youngest bulls begin growing their antlers last. The growth of a three- or four-year-old bull's antlers takes approximately 140 days; it takes only about 115 days for a two-year-old to grow his antlers. Bull elk will expend as much energy growing a new set of antlers as a cow will in growing her new calf.

While hunters are most concerned with bulls and their behavior, the cows actually control the day-to-day activities of the elk herd. Find the cows and the bulls are sure to be close by.

Antler growth is completed by August or early September. Bulls expend nearly as much energy growing antlers as cows do in growing their new calves.

As summer continues, elk are fat and sassy. Antler growth is completed by late August or early September. All elk are feeding heavily and putting on weight, spending 90 percent of their time either feeding or resting.

As August passes, bulls' testosterone levels begin to rise noticeably, and the breeding urge grows stronger by the day. Bulls will begin "raking" small trees both to scrape the velvet off their antlers and to mock battle movements they might have to use later.

The Wondrous Fall

The actual timing of the rut (breeding season) varies according to several factors, including climatic conditions and the condition of the animals. It generally occurs somewhere between late August and September, though some rutting activity can occur through October and on into early November. We'll take a more in-depth look at the rut in chapter five.

Following the rut, the elk once again split up—cows and calves go one way and mature bulls head another. At this time, the bulls can seemingly vanish from the face of the earth. Where do they go? Tired and battered from the rigors of a rut that can cost them as much as a third of their total body weight, bulls head for isolated pockets of deep cover where they will not be disturbed by man or beast. They need the quiet so they can regain their strength in anticipation of the coming winter. They may go hide in small groups of two to five bulls, or they may go off alone.

Cows and calves are feeding heavily now, spending lots of time in grassy meadows and parks as they, too, try to build strength for the challenge of winter.

Ol' Man Winter

As the days grow shorter and nights colder, elk begin thinking of migrating down out of the high country toward their low-elevation winter range. Elk usually follow traditional migration routes on this journey; however, most elk will not leave summer range until deep snow forces them to. In years of light snowfall, the migration can be delayed for days or even weeks. When early snows come, the elk may start traveling early. Nothing is set in stone.

Once the rut is completed, the worn-down bulls retreat to isolated pockets of deep cover where they rest and recuperate in anticipation of the coming winter.

When the snows get deep and temperatures plummet in winter, elk begin their migration to the low-elevation winter range. In winter, elk prefer to move as little as possible, conserving energy and concentrating on feeding enough to keep their inner fires stoked.

During winter, elk move as little as possible, conserving their energy and concentrating on feeding. They move only enough to find plenty to eat, or to find shelter during storms and strong winds.

The Rejuvenating Spring

When winter begins breaking sometime in March, elk are restless. They know that as the high meadows become exposed under the warm sun, a bounty of lush grasses and other forage will become available on their summer range. By late March, cows, calves and young bulls begin their trek back to the high country, again following traditional migration routes. The older, more mature bulls usually precede the other elk, their trek inhibited only by the snow depth. Once on the summer range, the cows will feed heavily in anticipation of their new calf crop, while the bulls will lounge and eat heavily too, as they wait for their new antlers to sprout forth.

Elk Habitat

To find elk, you have to know how to recognize the kinds of habitat they prefer and what they eat. The key—regardless of where elk live—is edge cover.

In mountainous country, prime elk habitat is characterized by timbered ridges pockmarked with grassy parks (open areas) and meadows of all shapes and sizes. In the Southwest, vast expanses of grassy plains are sliced by thick scrub brush and smaller trees, making good elk habitat. Coastal rain forest areas have their edge cover too, often consisting of meadows and parks.

Logging, when not done to excess, can create excellent edge cover for elk, with the new growth generated in the cut-over areas providing lots of nutritious food. Old burns are elk magnets. Edge cover can also be found inside the timber, of course, in the form of small meadows and stream banks.

Elk also need water, and plenty of it, especially in the hot weather of summer and early fall. Elk will drink from any available water source—including rivers and streams, lakes and ponds, small seeps and springs, and water tanks built by

Elk are creatures of "edge" habitat, which provides them with nutritious food, easy access to escape cover and comfortable travel routes. Grassy parks and meadows, as well as newly logged areas, can provide the kind of nutritious foods that elk need to pack on the pounds.

people. In arid regions like the Southwest, elk will travel miles each day to drink if they have to.

Comfortable resting areas are another must for a healthy elk herd. With their thick, long-haired hides, the hot sun can really cause them to overheat, so elk must have shaded areas in hot weather. They'll even lie in the shade on relatively warm days in the depths of winter. In early spring, before they've shed much of their winter coat, elk will often lie on or near receding snowbanks, trying to stay cool. They like to catch prevailing breezes during warm days and will often bed up on windward ridgetops for this reason. However, when hunting pressure occurs, elk like to bed in the dark timber, secure among the tangled blow-downs, deep canyons and brushy hillsides where only the hardiest and most dedicated hunters venture.

Learning to recognize elks' preferred foods in a given area will help you locate them too. Like cattle, elk are primarily grazers and love fresh grasses whenever possible. The amount of grass in an elk's diet depends on where it lives. A 1973 study by R. C. Kufield entitled "Foods Eaten by Rocky Mountain Elk" states that Montana has a tremendous amount of grassy meadows, and up to 84 percent of an elk's winter diet is grass. In Idaho, that total drops to 65 percent. In areas where grass is less abundant, like the Southwest, grasses may comprise as little as 22 percent of the elk's diet. When woody browse is prevalent, it can make up a significant portion of the elk's diet as well. Aspen, currant, snowberry, western juniper, serviceberry, huckleberry, bitterbrush, mountain mahogany and similar trees and shrubs are all part of an elk's diet from time to time. On a New Mexico hunt one year, I found that elk were eating the acorns from scrub oaks as fast as the trees dropped them.

But don't expect to see many elk—especially bulls—in open parks during daylight hours, especially during hunting seasons. Elk know the dangers of traveling in these open areas. That's why even though you might find tracks, droppings and resting beds in large parks, you'll rarely see any elk there. They enter parks to feed only after dark, and leave before the morning sun kisses the sky.

Bulls vs. Cows

While elk hunting is very different from most deer hunting, it is similar in that most hunters can find the females but have trouble locating the males. Understanding an elk's daily movement pattern will help you find the antlers you seek.

By nature, elk are restless animals, covering lots of ground each day in search of enough food to satisfy their large appetites. But once they have settled into a particular range, they move only as much as necessary to meet their physical needs. These natural movement patterns are affected by outside pressures—like quick weather changes and, of course, hunting pressure.

Generally speaking, elk begin their daily movement pattern in the late afternoon. From their bedding areas in the thick brush or dark timber they begin feeding downslope toward open meadows and parks containing the grasses on which they gorge themselves. Reaching these meadows just before dark, they'll feed there off and on all night, resting when not actively feeding. Then

Mature bulls are loners by nature, preferring solitude or the company of a handful of other bulls most of the year. Only during the rut are they found associating regularly with herds of cows.

just before daylight, they'll herd up and begin their march back up the slope to bedding areas reached by mid-morning, where they spend the day resting and ruminating.

The similarity in the patterns of both bulls and cows ends there. It is rare to find mature bulls with cows and calves except during the rut, which can last for up to two months. You can often find mature bulls on the fringes of herds of cows and calves. The bulls often live in country that is rougher and appears to be not as conducive to survival; indeed it is not. Because there are fewer bulls than cows in virtually all wild elk populations—and because it is nature's way to provide the very best food and water for the young, to whom it is much more critical for survival—bulls yield this prime habitat to the young and their mothers.

You'll often find bulls at the highest edges of good cover, living on the top edge of timberline. They also like to hang out in the dark, deep recesses of thick timber; at the bottoms of deep gorges and in heavily brushed ridges; blow-down hellholes; and other isolated pockets where they are disturbed little. In winter, bulls are often the last to leave the winter range, coming down out of the high country only when the snow gets belly deep.

It is important when searching for bulls to remember that elk are what we call "pocket" animals. That means that while there may be a large drainage of several square miles comprised of excellent elk habitat, at any one time the vast majority of the elk will be found only in small isolated "pockets" of this drainage. I can remember many an elk hunt when it took several days of hiking many miles each day up and down the mountains, as well as long hours of glassing during the "prime time" of dawn and dusk—before I found where the bulls were actually hanging out, in the midst of all that beautiful habitat.

Bulls like to hang on the upper edges of prime habitat; in dark, deep recesses of thick timber; at the bottoms of deep gorges and hellhole blowdowns; and along heavily brushed ridges.

AccuNav
SPORT
GPS
EAGLE
MADE IN U.S.A.

Chapter 2

Gearing Up

Let's face it—hunters like their "stuff." In the off-season there are few activities more enjoyable than shopping for new hunting equipment. Thumbing through the big mail-order catalogs is a must, of course, as is reading all about the latest gadgets and gizmos in the various sporting magazines. And when your buddies bring over something new that you don't have, well, that's when the fires really start burning.

Elk hunters definitely need the right stuff before heading afield. The right rifle, chambered for a cartridge more potent than your undersized deer rifle, is a great excuse for explaining that shiny new bolt gun to your spouse. What bowhunter among us can't use a new compound bow, another dozen arrows and the latest in broadhead technology? What about those new, powerful muzzleloading rifles? No use applying for a special blackpowder tag without one. Those mountain boots sure are looking worn out too. Probably should replace them. And one of those lightweight Gore-Tex rain suits certainly would be great. Oh, yeah. My daypack just isn't big enough for elk country, and I sure do need a pack frame stout enough to pack meat. After all, I am going to bag the biggest bull in the woods! What? That new GPS unit you saw in the garage? Well, you don't want me to get lost, do you?

One thing veteran elk hunters have learned—and learned the hard way, I assure you—is that while they need the right stuff in the elk woods, there can be too much of a good thing when it comes to packing all sorts of gadgets and gizmos up and down the steep elk mountains. Equipment needs to be chosen wisely—carefully balanced between what we'd like to have with us and what we really need to be comfortable, safe, successful elk hunters.

Here's how to separate the wheat from the chaff ...

Guns & Loads for Elk

"I don't understand all this talk about needing big guns for elk hunting," a friend from back East said. "Heck, bowhunters take elk all the time with their itty-bitty arrows."

True enough. And, in past years, so did folks shooting .30-30s and even old-style flintlock and percussion muzzleloaders. So why all the hoopla about using cartridges with so much oomph?

First off, elk are highly prized not just for their large sets of antlers and their physical size but also because they are such a tremendous challenge to hunt and because they are quite possibly the tastiest of all our ungulates on the dinner table. An elk in the freezer means a year or more of high-quality, low-fat meat for the family. It's a good feeling indeed.

Getting into position for a shot at a legal bull or cow elk is rarely easy. Often elk are

Elk hunters have a wide range of effective cartridges from which to choose, beginning with the .270 Win. on the bottom end of the scale. These six classic cartridges are all effective elk medicine. Clockwise from top: .270 Win., .280 Rem., .300 Win. Mag., .338 Win. Mag., 7mm Rem. Mag. and .30-06.

found in thick timber or brush, and shot angles are often less than ideal. Once you do get into position, you want to make sure you're packing a cartridge that can deliver enough punch to harvest the animal cleanly and humanely. This means stepping up into another class of cartridge from many acceptable deer rounds—necessary because not only are elk three to five times larger than the average deer, with much thicker hides and larger bones, but also because elk are arguably the toughest big-game animal in North America today, possessing a will to live unmatched by any other animal. No other animals I've hunted on the continent—including moose, mountain grizzly bears and Alaska's huge brown bears—are more tenacious to life than elk. You have to place your shot well, and use the right cartridge loaded with a top-quality bullet, to take elk cleanly. Hit poorly with the wrong bullet from a small cartridge, the average elk can travel miles over tough terrain and make recovery difficult at best.

Elk Cartridge Minimums and Maximums

First and foremost, never use anything but the best bullets you can buy when hunting elk. This means the so-called "premium" and "super premium" bullets like the Nosler Partition and Partition Gold, Barnes X-Bullet, Winchester Fail Safe, Trophy Bonded Bear Claw, Speer Grand Slam, Swift A-Frame and similar slugs costing a couple bucks apiece. Designed for deep penetration and controlled expansion, these bullets are tough enough to withstand impact with heavy elk bones and will still get to the vital area. Handloaders can find these bullets at will. Factory ammunition users can find them in select cartridges loaded by Federal, Remington, Winchester and Speer.

Craig Boddington, the well-known hunting writer and former editor of Petersen's *Hunting* magazine, is one of the most accomplished big-game hunters in the world today. "I like using as large a cartridge as is practical for elk,"

The ideal elk rifle is an accurate bolt gun that's light enough to pack for a week in steep, tough country and is chambered for the largest caliber the individual can shoot well. *The .270 is the absolute minimum, with the .30-06, various .300 magnums and the .338 Win. Mag. excellent all-around elk cartridges.*

Boddington comments. "I think the most important thing a person can do when choosing an elk cartridge is to use the largest caliber they can shoot well. It doesn't matter what you're shooting if you can't hit what you're aiming at because the recoil scares you into flinching."

The largest caliber they can shoot well. These are words to take to the bank, and not just when discussing elk hunting, but for all big-game hunting for that matter. The number-two complaint I hear from elk outfitters throughout the West about their clients—right after the client being physically unable to hike and climb the steep

Select Elk Cartridges

Cartridge Name	Bullet Wt.	Velocity (fps) Muzzle	100	200	300	400	Kinetic Energy (ft./lbs.) Muzzle	100	200	300	400
.270	150	2850	2504	2183	1886	1618	2705	2087	1587	1185	872
.280 Rem.	150	2890	2624	2373	2135	1912	2781	2293	1875	1518	1217
.280 Rem.	160	2840	2637	2442	2256	2078	2866	2471	2120	1809	1535
7mm Rem. Mag.	160	2950	2745	2550	2363	2184	3093	2679	2311	1984	1694
7mm Rem. Mag.	175	2860	2645	2440	2244	2057	3178	2718	2313	1956	1644
.308	180	2620	2274	1955	1666	1414	2743	2066	1527	1109	799
.30-06	180	2700	2348	2023	1727	1466	2913	2203	1635	1192	859
.300 Savage	180	2350	2025	1728	1467	1252	2207	1639	1193	860	626
.300 Win. Mag.	180	2960	2745	2540	2344	2157	3501	3011	2578	2196	1859
.300 Win. Mag.	200	2800	2570	2350	2150	1950	3480	2935	2460	2050	1690
.300 Wby. Mag.	180	3120	2866	2627	2400	2184	3890	3284	2758	2301	1905
.300 Wby. Mag.	200	2925	2690	2467	2254	2052	3799	3213	2701	2256	1870
8mm Rem. Mag.	200	2900	2623	2361	2115	1885	3734	3054	2476	1987	1577
.338 Win. Mag.	225	2800	2560	2330	2110	1900	3915	3265	2700	2220	1800
.338 Win. Mag.	250	2660	2400	2150	1910	1690	3925	3185	2555	2055	1590
.35 Whelen	250	2400	2197	2005	1823	1652	3197	2680	2230	1844	1515
.375 H&H Mag.	270	2690	2420	2166	1928	1707	4337	3510	2812	2228	1747

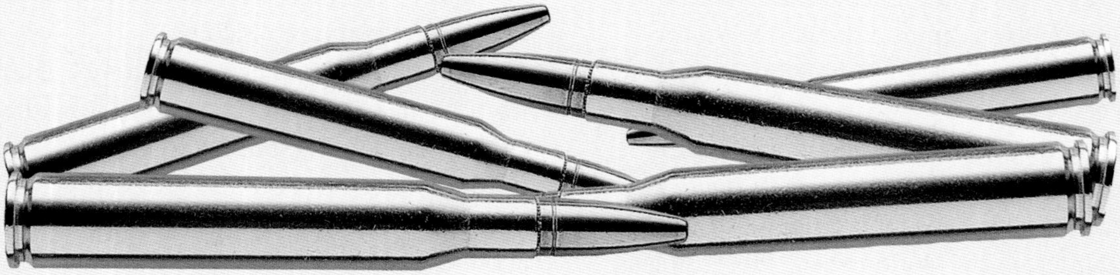

mountains—is that the hunters can't shoot their rifles, often because the weapon is in a cannon of a caliber that scares them into flinching.

With that in mind, let's look at minimums and maximums for an elk cartridge, trying to bridge the gap between having enough power and finding a caliber you can shoot well.

It is generally accepted that the minimum kinetic energy (K.E.) required to take elk-sized game is 1500 ft./lbs. at the target. That's a good reference point; however, kinetic energy doesn't tell us the whole story when it comes to elk hunting.

Rifle Actions

Caliber and cartridge selection is important, but so is your rifle's action. Best bet? A bolt. While a pump, lever or semi-automatic might seem good because it can throw a lot of lead, you're better off with the extra accuracy a bolt-action offers. Your first shot is the one that counts most, and many times shots at elk are on the long side (like 200 yards or more). Even if you do need follow-up shots, a bolt is just more reliable in the dust, dirt, snow, rain, cold and every other element that Western elk country dishes out.

Also important is using a relatively heavy bullet. Many small calibers, like the .270, .257 Roberts, .257 Weatherby Magnum and a host of others, achieve the 1500 ft./lbs. of K.E. value by pushing light bullets at extremely high velocity. And while this truckload of fine deer cartridges will take an elk cleanly if the distance and shot angle are right, I would not choose them for an elk hunt. What you want are relatively large-for-caliber bullets pushed along at moderate velocities. These are the bullets that deliver deep penetration regardless of the shot angle or distance, assuming the energy level is also there.

My own personal minimum for elk hunting is a premium-class 160- or 165-grain 7mm (.284 caliber) bullet. When loaded in the .280 Remington or in 7mm Remington and Weatherby Magnums, they are my minimum choice for elk hunting. These cartridges can get the job done even under marginal conditions, but they require surgical shot placement to do so.

The very best choice for elk hunting are premium-class bullets, which are designed to penetrate deeply and retain a high percentage of their original weight. Two excellent choices include the 180-grain .30-caliber Nosler Partition Gold (top) and 180-grain .30 caliber Winchester Fail Safe (bottom).

A big step up in performance on elk are certain .30 caliber cartridges. Most notable are the .30-06, .308 Winchester and .300 Savage using quality 180-grain bullets. These are fine elk rounds when shots are kept to moderate distances. The various .300 magnums are superb, especially out past 200 yards. Continuing up the ladder, we arrive at the real kings of elk hunting, the .338 Winchester and .340 Weatherby Magnums, using 225- and 250-grain bullets. These cartridges really produce some serious knock-down power as well as the flat trajectory to get the job done "way out there." Both the .35 Whelan and 8mm Rem. Mag. are also excellent elk medicine. The .375 H&H Mag. is another top-notch elk cartridge, but there's no need to own something *that* big unless you're first going to Africa or hunting Alaskan brown bear.

The accompanying chart (page 26) compares some of the better elk cartridges available today. When planning your elk hunting adventure, keep in mind that energy tables and ballistic charts are meaningless without accuracy. If big cartridges scare you—as they do many shooters—drop down a notch and use something with less recoil, like the .308 or .30-06. In elk hunting, as is the case in all big-game hunting, bullet placement is everything. The key to it all is bridging that gap between having a large-enough caliber you can shoot well and throwing a substantial slug that will penetrate well before expanding.

Archery Tackle for Elk

Elk are big, tough animals and tenacious to life like few others. Still, modern archery tackle is more than enough to meet the challenge. You just have to be able to get close enough to smell the elk's breath, be patient enough until the right shot opportunity—only broadside or quartering-away angles will do—and cool enough to be precise in placing your arrow at the moment of truth.

Bows for Elk

Too many bowhunters worry about raw arrow speed and forget about the importance of penetration, the need for reliability and the significance of quiet when choosing a compound bow for hunting. For elk hunting, it is better to have a bow that's forgiving and easy for you to draw and that consistently places the shaft on target at moderate

The keys to selecting the right archery gear for elk hunting are simplicity, strength and reliability. Bows must be smooth to draw, easy for you to hold for an extended period of time while at full draw and accurate. Broadheads must have strong, sharp blades. Both aluminum and carbon arrow shafts will do the job.

ranges ... than to have a whiz-bang speed bow that's noisy and groups arrows erratically.

Most important—you need a bow you can draw smoothly and hold for an extended period of time, in case your bull stops with brush or branches obscuring his chest. They do this a lot! You'll also be ahead of the game if you are able to draw and shoot from your knees or with your body twisted at an odd angle. And remember that shots can be on the long side, too. The first bull I shot with a bow was taken at 16 yards, but my longest shot on an elk brought down a large 5x5 bull at exactly 50 steps and was the only shot I had in a week of hard hunting. It will pay to tune your bow-and-arrow setup meticulously, then extend your own personal maximum shooting range prior to elk season.

Both one- and two-cam bows are excellent choices for elk hunting. Many industry experts who are also experienced elk bowhunters recommend a minimum draw weight of 60 pounds for men and 50 pounds for women for an elk-hunting bow. Because of the increased efficiency of today's bows, pulling Herculean draw weights isn't necessary to achieve relatively high arrow speed. Companies like Browning, Bear/Jennings, Custom Shooting Systems, Darton, High Country Archery, Hoyt, McPherson Archery, Mathews, Martin, Oneida, PSE and Xi, among others, all build quality bows suitable for elk hunting.

What about recurves? You bet! Many a good bull or fat cow elk fall to recurve bows each year, and top traditional bowhunters like Larry Jones and Fred Asbell consistently score with their recurves. If you're a traditional archer, there's no need to shy away from elk hunting.

Arrow Shafts & Broadheads

Both aluminum and carbon shafts are excellent elk-hunting arrows. I personally prefer hunting with carbon shafts, as I believe they are tougher and penetrate better than comparable aluminum shafts. That 50-yard bull described earlier was taken with a Gold Tip carbon shaft, which blew right through his chest and landed a good 20 yards on the other side of him. That said, I've taken over a dozen elk with aluminum arrow shafts. The bottom line is matching your shaft to your bow and shooting what you're comfortable with.

Elk have thick chests, heavy hides and big bones, all good reasons to use only quality broadheads with blades so sharp they scare you. I use replaceable-blade heads from companies like Barrie Archery, New Archery Products, Golden Key-Futura, Muzzy, Game Tracker, AHT and Archer's Ammo, and fixed-blade heads from companies like Elk Mountain Archery, Zwickey, Delta and Magnus. The key is a super-strong ferrule—like Barrie's titanium version—and strong blades. Some excellent elk hunters I know use mechanical broadheads from companies like Barrie Archery, Mar-Den, Sonoran Bowhunting Products, Game Tracker and New Archery Products, among others, with success.

Bow Sights

Your bow sight needs to be able to withstand some banging about; you'll undoubtedly knock it around on brush, rocks and other "gotchas." Fiber-optic sight pins are superb, as elk are often taken deep inside the dark timber or on the cusp of daylight. Make sure your bow sight has a rugged pin guard and a minimum of moving parts that can rattle loose, and that it can be secured tightly to the bow's riser. Sights from companies like Tru-Glo, Sight Master, Fine-Line, Browning, PSE, Sonoran Bowhunting Products, Jennings Archery, Cobra, Toxonics and Montana Black Gold are examples of good sights for elk hunting. Peep sights must let in maximum available light, too. Fine-Line's Sta-Brite, Game Tracker's Dusk Vision, the Shepley Peep and Shurz-A-Peep are all excellent.

Accessories

In my mind, a bow-attached quiver is the way to go for all Western hunting. Your arrows are conveniently at hand, and you won't have to worry about clanging and banging shafts noisily against brush like you will when wearing a hip quiver. Low-profile quivers like those from Sagittarius and Fine-Line are excellent.

Arrow rests can be another source of elk hunting frustration. Choose rests with the fewest moving parts, least number of screws and easiest adjustments. Golden Key-Futura, New Archery Products, Savage Systems and Bodoodle make excellent hunting rests.

I prefer wrist strap–type release aids, primarily because the strap keeps them from falling off when I'm moving quickly to get into position for a shot. There are many excellent releases out there, with those from Pro Release, Scott Archery, Golden Key-Futura, Jim Fletcher Archery, Tru-Fire, Winn Archery, Jerry Carter and T.R.U. Ball all excellent. Regardless of whether or not you shoot with a release or fingers, always carry a spare release or finger tab in your daypack or pants pocket ... just in case.

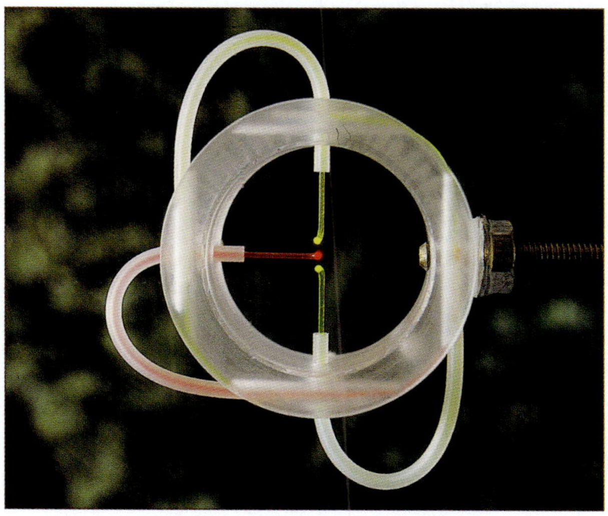

Bow sights with a minimum of screws, bolts and fragile parts that can rattle loose or break are far and away the top choice for elk hunting. Fiber-optic sight pins, like those found in this Tru-Glo sight, aid greatly in precisely placing arrows in the dim light when elk are most active.

Bowhunting for elk is one of the most challenging big-game hunting experiences you'll ever face. Take care to select matched tackle that has been precisely tuned and sighted in, then practice diligently, and when your binoculars are filled with a good bull, you can go after him confident you can make the shot at the moment of truth.

It's also advantageous to carry a couple of shafts tipped with either Judo or Bludgeon points, which I use for stump-shooting practice daily. A laser range finder, like the Bushnell Yardage Pro Compact 600 or Yardage Pro 400, can be a huge help in determining the exact distance to the target over the often-deceptive Western terrain. And something that makes it easy to check the wind constantly, like a butane lighter or a small puff bottle filled with unscented talc or corn starch, is essential. Unless you can beat the wind, and with it an elk's radar nose, you'll never have the chance to shoot a single arrow.

Blackpowder Bulls

While muzzleloader hunting has always had a following, its popularity increased with the growth in special muzzleloader-only hunts for deer and elk offered by many Western states. The purpose of these hunts, as far as game management officials were concerned, was to increase hunter participation without considerably increasing game harvest. At the same time special muzzleloader-only seasons took off, gun makers began offering a wide selection of top-quality, accurate muzzle-loading rifles at affordable prices. It's been a marriage made in heaven.

Most all Western elk states now offer at least a few muzzleloader-only elk hunts each fall, with tags generally available on a special-draw basis. To be successful when you're lucky enough to draw a coveted tag, you need "the right stuff" when it comes to muzzleloading rifles and accessories. Here's how to gear up.

From top: flintlock, sidelock and in-line muzzleloaders. Each have a place in elk country. While an accurate load for your particular muzzleloader is paramount, the rule of thumb in elk hunting is to use heavy bullets for caliber sent on their way by a maximum or near-maximum powder charge.

Rifles

Two types of muzzleloading rifles are most commonly seen in the elk woods each fall—sidelock and in-line. Both feature percussion-type ignition systems.

Sidelock percussion rifles are epitomized by the classic Hawken design and remain popular with traditionalists who want to step back in time and hunt elk the way the old-time trappers and explorers opening up the West did. Thompson/Center, CVA and Dixie Gun Works all make excellent rifles of this type.

Tony Knight, a gunsmith from Lancaster, Missouri, isn't concerned with tradition as much as functionality. He built the first modern in-line muzzleloading rifle in 1983. In 1985 he introduced the Knight MK-85, which set the tone for both the industry and the hunters it served. The MK-85 had modern rifle features, including receivers drilled and tapped for scope mounts and an adjustable trigger, plus a removable breech plug that greatly simplified cleaning and permitted hunters to push an unfired charge out the breech at day's end, instead of having to either pull the ball or bullet out the barrel or fire the rifle, which meant a half-hour's cleaning session back at home or camp. Other makers like White, Thompson/Center and CVA soon jumped on the bandwagon. Today a raft of additional companies—including Traditions, Gonic Arms, Markesbery Muzzleloaders, Navy Arms, Dixie Gun Works, Austen & Halleck, Remington, Ruger, Mossberg and Marlin—all sell quality in-line muzzleloaders.

In-lines are the best choice for serious, no-nonsense elk hunting. But because of their accuracy and effectiveness, Colorado has banned their use in muzzleloader-only seasons as of this printing. Before planning an elk hunt with an in-line, be sure to check state regulations.

As far as caliber goes, .50 caliber is the minimum choice; .54 caliber is even better. Regardless of which you choose, the most important thing is to work up an accurate load, learn to shoot the rifle well and get as close as possible before squeezing the trigger.

Bullets & Powder

While the patched round ball is still shot by

some, most muzzleloading elk hunters use either conical bullets or, where legal, sabot-encased conicals. These bullets provide plenty of penetration and kinetic energy for clean kills on the toughest old bulls. There are many different companies offering quality muzzleloading bullets today, including well-known blackpowder rifle makers like Thompson/Center, CVA, Traditions, Knight Rifles and Remington, as well as specialists like Buffalo Bullet Co., Muzzleload Magnum Products (MMP), Precision Rifle Bullets, Northern Precision, Parker Productions, Black Belt Bullets from Big Bore Express and Game Buster Bullets, and well-known and easily recognizable centerfire ammunition and bullet makers like Hornady, Barnes, Nosler, Swift Bullet Co. and Lyman.

The propellant choices are two—traditional blackpowder or Pyrodex, a synthetic propellant that performs like blackpowder. Goex and Elephant Blackpowder are the two most popular brands of traditional powder. However, today most muzzleloaders choose Hodgdon's Pyrodex, which is available in both traditional granulated form and Pyrodex Pellets, a premeasured charge that comes compressed in easy-to-use pellet form. Pyrodex Pellets are my first choice, hands down; however, synthetic propellants are not legal in all states, so be sure to check the regulations.

While an accurate load for your particular muzzleloader is paramount, the rule of thumb in elk hunting is to use heavy bullets for caliber sent on their way by a maximum or near-maximum powder charge.

Accessories

Muzzleloader hunters require their own specialized accessories for cleaning and loading their rifles and packing their stuff.

Most blackpowder rifle makers offer cleaning supplies like ramrods and attachments, patches and cleaning solvents, often packaging them in kit form. These and other items like powder measures, powder flasks, speed loaders, percussion caps, cappers, possible bags and pouches and other accessories are offered by many major gun makers but also by well-known aftermarket accessory manufacturers like Uncle Mike's and Bridgers Best. One excellent accessory item is the Dry Fire Breech Protector, a simply designed product that keeps moisture out of the breech area of many models of in-line muzzleloaders. Another is the Traditions EZ Unloader, which uses a blast of compressed air at the breech end to push powder and projectile down and out the barrel when unloading at day's end.

Taking it one step further, many experienced shooters are looking to upgrade their sighting systems. TruGlo's excellent fiber-optic Illuminator, Muzzle Dot and Magnum Muzzle Dot sights are superb choices for hunting with open sights. Some rifle makers offer them as standard fare, and you can also get them as aftermarket replacement parts. Williams Gun Sight Company's Firesight is another fiber-optic sight that is made of steel, not plastic. Some hunters replace their factory open sights with a peep sight like Thompson/Center's Tang Peep Sight. And while some optics manufacturers like Burris, Bushnell, Leupold and Simmons produce scopes touted specifically for modern muzzleloaders, many in-line shooters top their rifles with the same top-quality variable rifle scope they use on their centerfire rifles. Scopes are not legal in all states, so be sure to check regulations before adding one.

Heading Afield

When heading afield, keep it simple. I carry five preloaded speed loaders filled with premeasured Pyrodex charges or pellets and bullets, a short starter and a full capper. I also pack a combination nipple/breech plug wrench, several clean, pre-lubed patches and a small amount of bore cleaner should I have to clean the rifle in the field. I also pack a couple of small balloons that can be fitted over the barrel if it starts raining. That's it. Everything else, including a spare ramrod and full cleaning kit, stays at base camp.

Muzzleloaders—Equipment Checklist

- ☑ Rifle
- ☑ Percussion caps
- ☑ Capper
- ☑ Blackpowder or Pyrodex
- ☑ Powder measure
- ☑ Powder flask
- ☑ Bullets
- ☑ Short bullet starter
- ☑ Synthetic ramrod
- ☑ Nipple/breech plug wrench
- ☑ Pre-lubed patches
- ☑ Bullet lube
- ☑ Speed loaders
- ☑ Small balloons (for barrel protection)
- ☑ Cleaning supplies (powder solvent, clean patches, ramrod attachments, light gun oil)

Backpacking for Elk

I started backpacking for elk a long time ago, tired of seeing more hunters than elk on hunts near roads. Being a college student who could barely afford a nonresident elk tag and the gas money to get from California to Colorado, I needed the cheapest way to access backcountry areas where horseback riders and outfitted hunters were shooting all the bulls. My first backpack elk hunt was quite the learning experience. I got a quick graduate degree in hard work, being lucky enough to shoot a small bull "only" five miles from the road. It took three days to get all the meat out, and when it was all over I was beat up a lot worse than at the end of the first session of two-a-days during football practice.

But I was hooked! Here was a way to get into the best hunting for minimal money. And even today, the feeling of accomplishment following a successful backpack hunt remains unsurpassed.

One fact I've learned over the years is that consistently successful public-land elk hunters know they must get away from other hunters whenever possible. Those who pay the price in sweat equity have a much better chance of bagging an elk than those who stick to the roads. On do-it-yourself hunts, I've tried escaping crowds two ways. Every now and then, I'll leave my roadside camp shortly after midnight and climb high up timbered ridges, hoping to be in position at the crack of dawn. I'll hunt hard in the morning, take a nap at midday, then hunt hard until dark, making my way back down the mountain by flashlight.

The best way, however, is to backpack camp and all into the wilderness, bringing enough food and gear to stay a week or more. While backpacking is hard work (and getting harder every year as my bones grow older), it is still the least expensive way to give yourself a better-than-average chance at an elk.

Consistently successful public-land elk hunters know that they must get away from the crowds to find elk to hunt. Backpacking camp into out-of-the-way areas is a great way to locate isolated, elk-rich pockets.

There are other chapters in this book that apply to backpack hunting, notably sections on physical conditioning, mental toughness, researching the hunt and meat care. So here we'll focus on the equipment you'll need to make backpack hunting a realistic option. When selecting backpack hunting gear, remember the phrase "performance without weight." You need gear that will get the job done without an extra ounce ... which would make an already difficult job even tougher.

The Hunting Pack

Elk hunters need a stout backpack with a large bag, both to carry their camp and gear into the woods and to pack meat and antlers back to the road. If you haven't looked at backpacks in a few years, you'll be amazed at how they keep evolving. Companies like Camp Trails, Badlands, Kelty, Lowe Alpine Systems and Dana Designs are producing the finest high-volume, lightweight packs ever made.

Your pack bag needs plenty of outside pockets for stuffing items like water bottles, a first aid kit, maps and the like. The frame must have a harness system designed for heavy loads, be adjustable so it can be fitted exactly to your body, and feature triple-stitching that won't rip out when the going gets tough. You'll also need to get a rain cover for your pack—a cover costs only about 20 bucks—to keep it dry.

I also like to bring along a fanny pack or daypack, which I use as my daily hunting pack. That way I can move easier, quieter (be sure to use a pack with a soft, quiet fabric on the outside) and with less weight through the elk woods than when carrying my haul-everything pack and bag. Fieldline, Crooked Horn Outfitters and White Buffalo Outdoors make excellent packs for this job. I store everything inside my packs in either a heavy-duty trash bag or zip-top baggies to help keep everything both dry and dust-free.

Gimme Shelter

You need to have adequate shelter when backpacking. Regardless of where or when you hunt, you can count on at least part of the trip involving rain, snow or high winds—or all three. In addition, you have to sleep comfortably and well to allow your body to recover from the rigors of wilderness hunting on foot. Yet camp can't weigh a ton. My own three-season tent, sleeping bag and pad together weigh just 9 pounds and have kept me warm and dry in heavy rains, winds of over 75 miles per hour, deep snows and temperatures near 0°F. A space blanket can serve as an emergency shelter and, together with parachute cord, can be rigged into a small lean-to for cooking, drying wet clothes and sitting up outside the tent in the evening.

You Gotta Eat

While I eliminate ounces in my backpacking gear, the one area where I won't scrimp is food. Wilderness hunting is hard work, and your body needs plenty of calories to keep it going. On hunts of a week or more, I pack one freeze-dried dinner per person per day. Breakfast is built around instant oatmeal, while midday meals and snacks are centered around jerky and granola bars. I always pack some dried fruit and Carbo Fuel, a concentrated carbohydrate powder that, when mixed with water, helps boost your energy level during strenuous exercise. I've also packed tubes of peanut butter, a roll or two of bagels, a brick of cheese and some hard candies. And I always take a multi-vitamin tablet each day.

My kitchen consists of a small backpack stove, filled fuel bottle, small aluminum coffee pot for boiling water, a Lexan spoon and fork, and two quart-sized water bottles that I pack hunting each day. You can eat the freeze-dried dinners right from the pouch; I cook the oatmeal in the coffee pot.

The secret is to bring foods that are high in calorie content per ounce yet also provide proper nutrition. Figure that you'll need to pack somewhere between 1½ to 2 pounds of food per person per day on a backpack hunt.

Where Can I Find This Stuff?

The best place to find cutting-edge tents, sleeping bags, backpacks and other state-of-the-art backpacking equipment—plus personnel knowledgeable in the use of this equipment—is a specialty backpacking or mountaineering store. Some large mail-order hunting companies and a few large hunting stores carry some backpacking equipment, but they can't beat the specialty shops for this kind of equipment or expert help in selecting the right gear.

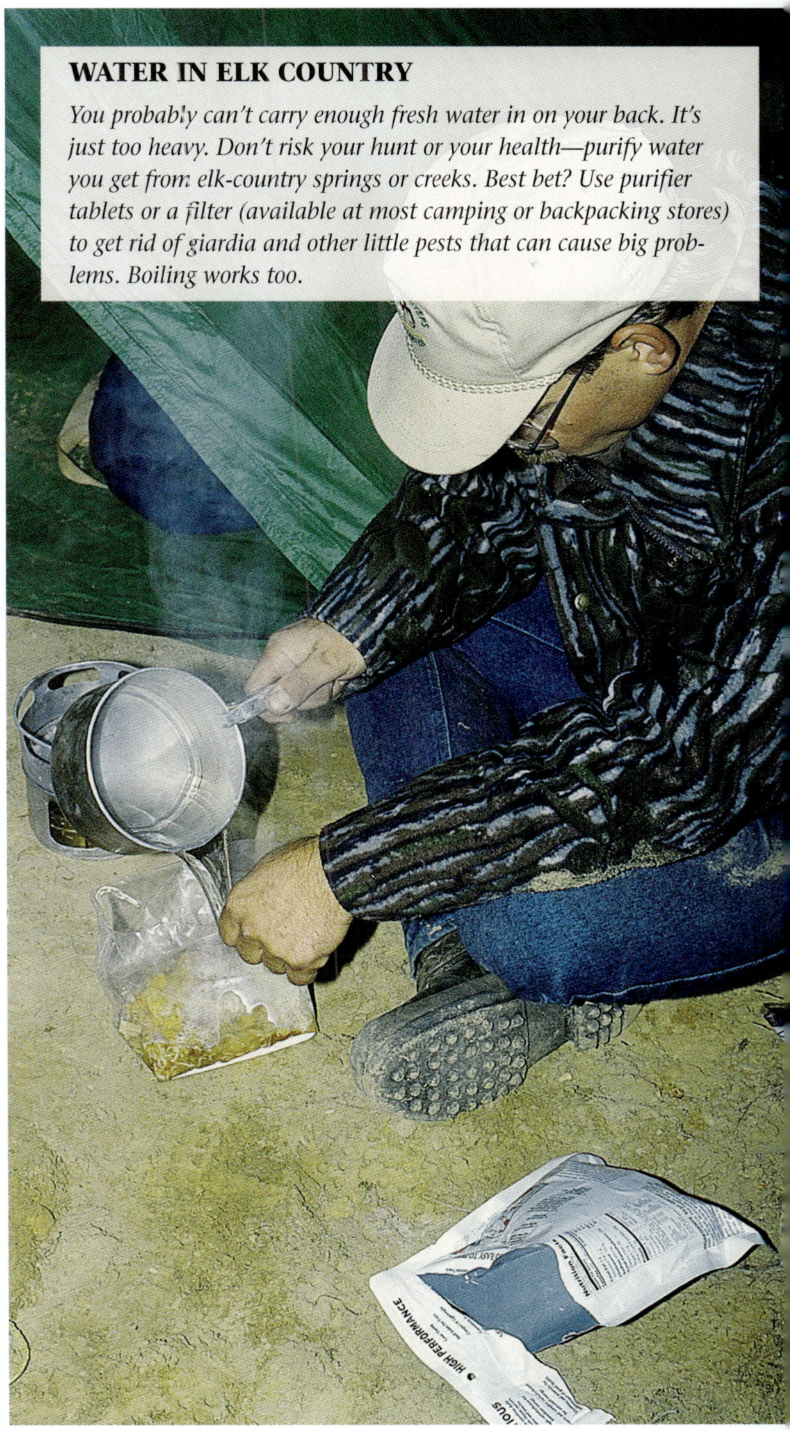

WATER IN ELK COUNTRY

You probably can't carry enough fresh water in on your back. It's just too heavy. Don't risk your hunt or your health—purify water you get from elk-country springs or creeks. Best bet? Use purifier tablets or a filter (available at most camping or backpacking stores) to get rid of giardia and other little pests that can cause big problems. Boiling works too.

Backpacking—Equipment Checklist

- ☑ Backpack and rain cover
- ☑ Daypack or fanny pack
- ☑ Spare pack pins
- ☑ Tent with rainfly
- ☑ Sleeping bag
- ☑ Sleeping pad
- ☑ Space blanket
- ☑ Stove
- ☑ Filled fuel bottle
- ☑ Cooking pot (coffee pot)
- ☑ Lexan spoon, fork
- ☑ Quart-sized water bottles (2)
- ☑ Food (1½ to 2 pounds per person per day)
- ☑ Waterproof matches or butane lighter
- ☑ Nylon parachute cord (50 feet)
- ☑ Toilet paper
- ☑ Small hand towel
- ☑ Liquid camp soap
- ☑ Hunting knife, whetstone
- ☑ Compact bone saw
- ☑ Headlamp, new batteries
- ☑ Fluorescent flagging (½ roll)
- ☑ First aid kit
- ☑ 1-inch cloth athletic tape, small roll
- ☑ Moleskin
- ☑ Game bags (4)
- ☑ Water purification tablets
- ☑ Compass, topographic maps
- ☑ Heavy-duty 33-gallon trash bags (2)
- ☑ Hunting license, elk tag

The Daypack

Elk hunters need a large-volume daypack, with the emphasis on *large*. Why? Depending on the time of year, on wilderness elk hunts you'll need to carry an assortment of bulky gear that includes a rain suit; warm jacket, hat and gloves; lunch and water. This is in addition to all the other "everyday" hunting stuff you'll need to have along.

A top-notch hunting daypack will feature an outer shell material of either polar fleece or one of the new soft, quiet nylon fabrics like Stealth Cloth that are whisper-quiet when going through brush. It will have large, adjustable shoulder straps to help evenly distribute weight, an easily adjustable waist belt and chest strap that both feature quick-detach buckles of high-impact plastic, side pockets large enough for a water bottle or spotting scope, plus smaller pockets for smaller items. Some top-quality daypacks feature a leather or reinforced bottom pad to guard against wear and tear. A waterproof liner inside the main compartment is useful. Companies like Fieldline, Crooked Horn Outfitters, Badlands and White Buffalo Outdoors make excellent daypacks, as do mail-order houses Cabela's and Bass Pro Shops.

Make sure your daypack's shoulder straps can be snugged firmly up against your shoulders. For some reason many pack designers build their packs for oversized men with weightlifter chests. Unless the pack can be cinched tightly on your body frame, carrying heavy loads will be uncomfortable and unnecessarily fatiguing.

Deciding what to carry in your daypack can vary depending on the time of year, the terrain being hunted and whether or not you're hunting alone. Basic survival items should always go with you whenever you step into the elk woods. The rest can be added and subtracted depending on the time of year. My daypack first aid items are minimal, but I always have more extensive items in base camp just in case.

Daypack Essential: GPS Unit

One accessory I consider a necessity in today's elk hunting is a GPS unit. From scouting to hunting to finding your way back to camp or your vehicle, these units are invaluable.

A compact GPS unit can be a valuable aid in wilderness hunting, making it easy to relocate areas of hot sign and find your way back to camp after dark.

Scouting with GPS Units

When scouting, you can save the locations of important sightings like rubs, wallows, waterholes, game trails and preferred food sources into your GPS unit. Later, in the comfort of your home or camp, you can match these sightings and their locations with topographic maps to plot their locations in conjunction with topography, roads and so on. Using these observations can help you analyze what's happening in a given area at a given time and can help you organize a well-thought-out hunting strategy that meets those conditions.

Hunting with GPS Units

There are a million-and-one possible uses for a GPS unit in elk hunting. Here are a few examples.

Finding camp after dark can be a tough proposition, especially on wilderness hunts where there are few trails, fewer roads and no lights. By marking camp on the GPS unit before leaving to hunt during the day, you can hunt relatively worry-free, then use the unit to navigate back to camp after dark with no trouble at all.

If you've taken an elk far from the road or camp, using the GPS unit is a no-brainer. It used to be that we'd have to leave a trail of fluorescent flagging to follow back to the carcass, then we'd worry both about packing out the animal and picking up the flagging as we left the area. Now just save the exact location of the carcass into the GPS unit's memory, and you can return to the site any time you want without all the flagging.

This may seem like a small thing. But if you're like me, you are more than a little secretive about places where hard-won successes have come. I don't want to leave a flagging trail that someone else might stumble onto, then bring his entire crew of buddies to hunt my secret area. With my flagless GPS trail, I don't have to worry about that anymore.

The Future of GPS Units

GPS unit use is sure to grow as more and more people become familiar with them, learn how simple they really are to operate and recognize the decrease in both their size and cost. Even though I write on a word processor, I'm computer illiterate, and using all this high-tech electronic

GPS Units and Elk Hunting

The Global Positioning System, or GPS, is a highly accurate navigational system developed by the United States Department of Defense that can be used anywhere in the world. It is based on a group of 21 working satellites, plus 3 in-orbit spares. Precise orbits of each satellite assure that at least 4 are in view at all times from any position on the face of the earth. Because of the satellites and the sophisticated receivers that we use in conjunction with them, GPS units can be used 24 hours a day, in virtually all weather conditions.

GPS works by measuring the time it takes a radio signal to reach the receiver from a satellite, converting that time into distance and then determining exactly how far it is from the transmitting satellite. By measuring the distance from 3 of the 4 satellites always in view, a position can be fixed in latitude and longitude. It's a "Star Trek" way of using the ancient method of triangulation to fix a position using landmarks that include everything from rocks and trees to the stars themselves. And by reading the 4th satellite—the one most directly overhead—the GPS unit can give you your current altitude. One of the real advantages of this kind of navigation system is the fact that you can use it to get from point A to point B time after time, even in the dark. This can be done during scouting trips or the actual hunt itself. And you can save waypoints and coordinates from your own hunting or scouting and pass them along to a buddy, and he can go back to the exact spot you did, even if you're not there, by plugging the coordinates into his own GPS unit.

stuff is intimidating to me. But I've found that programming most GPS units is as close to a no-brainer as anything of its kind I've ever used. It's literally easier than programming your VCR!

GPS units are here to stay. They're easy to use and as reliable as the sunrise. GPS units are tools that can not only help you become more successful but let you have more fun in the woods too. Take a close look at them at your local dealer, and you'll see what I mean.

Daypack Items

- ☑ Hunting license, elk tag
- ☑ Quart-sized water bottle
- ☑ Compass with mirror
- ☑ GPS unit
- ☑ Topographic maps
- ☑ Butane lighter or waterproof matches
- ☑ Firestarter material
- ☑ Space blanket
- ☑ Flashlight or headlamp, fresh batteries
- ☑ Hunting knife, whetstone
- ☑ Nylon parachute cord (50 feet)
- ☑ Assorted Band-Aids
- ☑ 1-inch cloth athletic tape (small roll)
- ☑ Moleskin
- ☑ Ibuprofen tablets
- ☑ Personal medications
- ☑ Spare eyeglasses
- ☑ Lunch/snacks
- ☑ Toilet paper
- ☑ Fluorescent flagging (½ roll)
- ☑ Change of socks

During late season, add:

- ☑ Warm gloves
- ☑ Stocking cap
- ☑ Light vest or jacket
- ☑ Packable Gore-Tex rain suit

Dress for Success

During the course of a long elk season, hunters can experience extremes from hot and dry to cold and rainy to frigid sleet and snow. To be able to hunt at peak efficiency, you have to dress for success.

It is important to think of your hunting clothing as a system, in which all the parts work together to provide a microclimate against your body that keeps it warm but not too hot, cool but not too cold and protects it against the elements. To that end, choose garments designed for the conditions at hand.

The Importance of Layering

Rather than wear one heavy jacket over a thin shirt, it is better to wear several thinner garments that can be removed and/or vented when you're too hot, then be put back on or closed up when you're too cold. For example, hiking up a steep mountainside will make the body hot, so you need layers on top that can either be removed and carried or zipped open or unbuttoned to allow body heat to escape.

Your first layer should be a wicking-type synthetic underwear of polypropylene, Thermax, Coolmax or other high-tech fabric that both insulates and keeps moisture vapor—sweat—off the body. Removing this moisture is the key to staying comfortable. Cotton long johns—which lose their insulative values when wet with sweat or due to the elements—are a definite no-no.

What to Wear

Under layers: Capilene or Thermax long johns, wicking socks. Thorlo, Whitewater Outdoors and Wigwam make good hiking and hunting socks.

Always use fleece or other quiet fabrics as your outer layer. No exceptions.

Outer Layers: Silence is the bottom line. During the early season, fleece pants and jackets are excellent. Later on, wool pants and shirts or Gore-Tex fleece pants and jackets are super. The new Gore Windstopper shirt from Whitewater Outdoors is lightweight, windproof and made from silent Stealth Cloth; it helps eliminate additional layers. Add or subtract layers as conditions dictate.

Footwear: Bob-type soles offer excellent traction. Gore-Tex boots are waterproof and breathable. Choose the insulation type based on weather and time of year. Rubber-bottom, leather-upper pac boots are best for the cold and deep snow of very late seasons.

Head & Hands: Billed cap, stocking cap and gloves are necessary. During bow season, don't forget a head net or CarboMask face paint. Thin polypropylene glove liners are valuable.

Rainwear: With silent outer fabric, the new lightweight, packable Gore-Tex rain suits from Whitewater Outdoors, 10X and Cabela's are superb for active elk hunting.

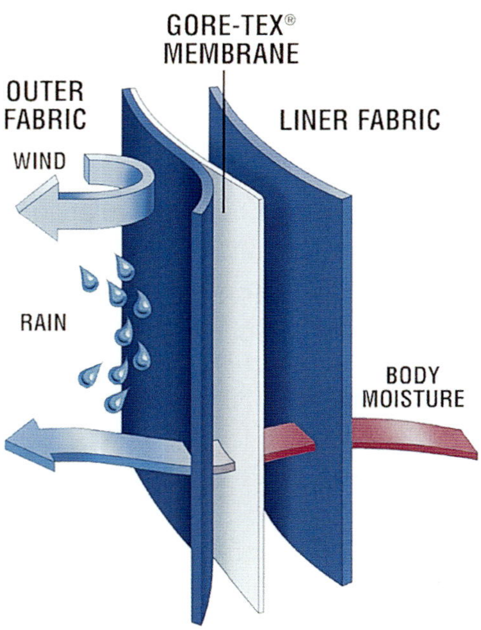

Gore-Tex and Windstopper outerwear is both waterproof and windproof, and it also "breathes," allowing sweat to escape as moisture vapor. These high-tech garments can help make you a more efficient elk hunter. Art courtesy of W. L. Gore & Associates.

Outerwear

Add subsequent layers of breathable materials that continue to permit moisture vapor to escape to the outside of the clothing system. Fleece, wool and synthetic materials will do this. Your outerwear must do two things: protect you from brush, rocks and other obstacles as well as the elements, and it must also be quiet. Noise is one reason smart elk hunters never wear scratchy nylon or denim and instead select fleece, wool or synthetics with a "soft hand." Scratch the material with your fingernails. If you can hear anything, know that an elk a football-field away will as well.

Two breathable high-tech materials that also block 100 percent of the wind and are laminated to many different outerwear shell fabrics are Gore-Tex and Windstopper. Gore-Tex is also 100 percent waterproof and can be found in superb lightweight, packable rain suits from companies like Whitewater Outdoors, Browning and 10X, among others, as well as in pants, jackets and hunting boots. Windstopper is designed for active hiking. I've found that wearing lightweight Windstopper shirts, gloves and caps actually allows me to wear fewer layers than in the "old days" before this laminate became available. That translates into less weight and bulk and, as a result, a more comfortable and efficient hunter.

Footwear

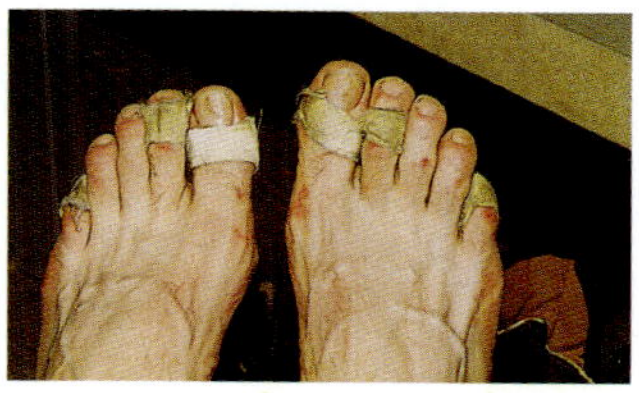

Here's what happens to your feet on a hard, long elk hunt. Imagine what the author's feet would have looked like if his boots hadn't *been broken in!*

Elk hunting boots must be rugged enough to offer ankle support and withstand the abuse of the toughest terrain, yet also breathe and remain waterproof. Gore-Tex boots with aggressive bob-type soles are the finest all-around, all-season elk hunting boots ever made. They are breathable, waterproof and tough. Companies like Danner, Georgia Boot, Wolverine, Rocky Boots and Northlake build excellent boots of this type. During early bow seasons some archers prefer lightweight canvas shoes or low-cut boots.

In the dead of winter, pac-type boots are the way to go. Schnee's, Hodgman, LaCrosse, Rocky Boots and Sorel make excellent winter hunting boots.

No matter what you wear, though, make sure that you break in the boots first by using them—and climbing in them—before you hunt. Elk hunting is pure hell on feet, and you don't need to be nursing blisters from stiff, unbroken boots; you'll have sore enough feet the way it is.

Head & Hands

The body loses more body heat from the head than from any other place. Don't overlook protecting both the head and hands in cool weather. Carrying a stocking-type cap and pair of light gloves in the daypack will allow you to stay warm while glassing from high atop a windy ridge. If you need a brim to block sun, adjust your baseball-style cap and place it right over the stocking cap. In winter, of course, heavier hats and gloves are essential; once again, *quiet* is the watchword.

Chapter 3

Heart & Soul

Have you ever been tired? Not just sleepy-time tired, but tired to the bone? So physically tired you can hardly put one foot in front of the other? So tired you begin to doubt whether or not you can take the next step? How about mentally tired? So frazzled you can hardly think, so ragged you begin making poor decisions about the simplest things, like where to place your foot for the next step?

Wilderness elk hunting will do all of that to you, and then some.

Elk hunting is, without question, damn hard work. The steep mountains, the sheer vastness of the country and the elk's ability to traverse miles of this type of terrain as easily as you walk down the street ... all are hard on even an elk hunter with the toughness of youth.

Also, the hours are long, with sleep not coming in peaceful eight-hour blocks but in short stretches of a few hours at a time. You have to be out hunting during "prime time"—at the crack of dawn and with the last wisps of light before dark—which means leaving camp well before it gets light and getting back well after the stars are out. On many an elk hunt lasting a week or more, the only time I actually see my camp in the daylight is when I set it up the day I get there and when I take it down the day I leave. Throw in bad weather and a few of the other things that simply break or go wrong in the backcountry, and you're in for a real test.

But these are the things that make elk hunting so special. It will test you, body and soul, like few other challenges you'll ever face. So you must prepare yourself, both physically and mentally, if you want to enjoy your time afield and give yourself a decent chance at success.

Anyone can do it, regardless of age. Even you. Here's how ...

Physical Conditioning

To be a consistently successful elk hunter, you have to be tough.

No, you don't have to be a world-class marathon runner or triathlete to get the job done. But you do have to be able to hike around some of North America's most challenging terrain, often at high altitude, for several days on end without lots of rest.

Fear not. Even couch potatoes can do it if they get themselves ready.

Mountain Shape

Each year I speak with hundreds of prospective elk hunters. Many live in the Midwest and East, where the country is smaller in every sense of the word. When I tell them about the vastness of public elk lands, the steep mountains and the high elevations, they nod their heads like they comprehend. Many have never met a meal they didn't like, and many have never been west of the Mississippi River. When they tell me they'll get in shape for elk hunting, most actually believe it.

They really don't have a clue when I tell them that it is impossible to be in too good of shape for elk hunting. All things being equal, hunters in

The best elk hunters are physically able to hike and climb many miles each day in search of pockets of elk. That means preparing your body well to handle the rigors of the hunt before you ever reach elk country.

top shape have a better chance of taking any elk than those who are not, for a variety of reasons. For Westerners, this holds true as well. Maybe even more so, because the natives are less likely to be hunting with an outfitter. I say these things not to offend, but to spur you to accept the challenge: *Get in shape.*

Why? Because elk are, by nature, herd animals. Even in the best elk country, elk herds are concentrated in a small portion of the available habitat. Like $e = mc^2$ you can bet on finding the most elk in areas farthest from the roads. Hunters in good shape can simply cover more country than those in poor condition; this in turn increases their odds for locating a herd of elk. Also, those in better shape can hunt the toughest parts of a given range—areas where the better bulls like to hang out once the shooting starts. While fatigue can't be avoided on an elk hunt, it will affect those in good shape less. Just as important, hunters in good shape will enjoy their wilderness experience even more.

Aerobic Conditioning

Aerobic means "with oxygen." When you're elk hunting, your body will process as much oxygen as it can. That means you need to train to improve your aerobic capacity.

High altitude is probably the most underrated oxygen-stealers there is. This is especially true for those who live in the low-elevation East. For

This is what elk hunting is all about—traversing the steep, tough country that elk frequent. Hunters in the best shape have the best chance at success.

example, the highest point in Pennsylvania is less than 3,500 feet. The lowest point in all of Colorado is 3,350 feet. With few exceptions, all Western elk hunting is done at a minimum of 5,000 feet, often between 7,000 and 10,000 feet. Even well-conditioned low-country lungs have trouble straining oxygen from this thin air. The bottom line is this: Wherever you hunt elk, whether on your own or with the services of an outfitter, you need to strengthen your legs, lungs and heart. That means aerobic exercise.

The first step is to visit your doctor for a checkup. Once he or she clears you to begin your program, there are several ways to get started. The easiest is to visit a local health club, gym or YMCA and enroll in some sort of aerobics class. There are several that will help you build a strong aerobic base. Aerobic dance and step classes are excellent. Jogging, bicycling and swimming are superb. Jumping rope is hard to beat.

One advantage to beginning at a health club or gym is that you can take advantage of the services of trained fitness professionals. They can explain to you how to determine your maximum heart rate and, from that, your training heart rate. They can also help you monitor your progress and set up a program designed to meet your fitness goal.

Specificity Training—Your Legs

Your goal is to be able to hike steep mountain country with a light pack on. To achieve this, you need to employ specificity training, a term athletes use to describe training for a specific event. For example, sprinters don't lift a lot of weights with their upper bodies; instead, they concentrate on training their legs, lungs and heart primarily by running or bicycling. You should do the same.

The best exercise of all for hiking the mountains is to carry a weighted daypack and to walk hilly country quickly. If no steep hills are close by, walk quickly up and down stadium steps or the stairs at work. In the gym, do leg exercises with weights. This will give you the strength to hike and climb. Coupled with exercises that increase aerobic capacity—like jogging, swimming, bicycling and jumping rope—you'll build a base of aerobic fitness and strength in the specific muscle groups you'll use most when elk hunting.

Weight Training

While not as important as aerobic conditioning and specificity training, employing a program of weight training will supplement your conditioning and make you all the tougher once you're in the mountains. The stronger your upper body is, the easier it will be for you to carry your pack all day long, pack out meat and antlers and do all those physical things that pop up during the course of mountain hunting. My own training program includes both upper-body weight training and aerobic exercise focused on climbing.

Let's Go Get 'Em!

At times, exercise is boring. Your body is sore and you just don't want to put on the togs and get with it. When I feel like that, I try to focus on the purpose of all this hard work. I envision the beautiful wilderness, the steep mountains and the majestic six-point bull elk I hope to get this year. I know that unless I get in shape, my chances for success are lessened. That helps keep me motivated through sore muscles, hectic work schedules and the demands of family and friends.

More importantly, as a fit individual you'll not only be a healthier person, you'll also enjoy your elk hunt to the fullest. With your mind totally focused on the task at hand, when your guide or hunting buddy says that the trophy of your dreams is just over the next ridge, you'll simply say, "We ain't there yet!" and not, "I can't make it."

The Case for Training

Here's a typical comment—these are the hunter's actual words—on being in shape *all over* for elk hunting. "I'm from Minnesota. Before my first elk hunt, I ran and ran and ran—I could run 7 or 8 miles in an hour, every day, no problem. Then I hit the mountains. My lungs were fine, but my flatlander's leg muscles weren't ready for climbing. I had the wind, but sometimes I didn't think my legs would budge again at the end of each day. Next time I'll hit the stairs in my training."

Specificity training is the way to get in shape for elk hunting. Replicating the activity you'll do most—hiking steep hills with a full daypack—will train your body specifically to handle the demands of steep, high-elevation Western mountains.

Mind over Matter

The odds are against you when you go elk hunting. In most states, success rates on general bulls-only hunts are below 25 percent—and sometimes only half that. This means that on a typical elk hunt, you're going to be spending a lot more time looking for elk than looking at elk. There may be several days when you don't see any elk at all, let alone a legal bull.

Anyone can keep his or her head in the game when there are lots of elk to look at. When someone gets lucky and shoots a bull early in the hunt, it's easy to be upbeat and excited. But when the hunting gets tough, when the elk seem to vanish into thin air, when the weather turns nasty and when you're tired and sore and hungry, it gets a lot harder to keep that excitement going.

That's where mental toughness comes in.

The Importance of PMA

A positive attitude is always important in hunting, but especially so when searching for elk. Hunters with PMA—Positive Mental Attitude—are always willing to climb one more mountain or dive into one more stand of dark timber than those who are down in the mouth and ready to give up. Those with PMA are much more fun to have in camp, adding to the total elk hunting experience. One bad attitude can bring down the entire camp, and when that happens, everyone suffers.

I vividly remember an archery elk hunt I took one September in southwestern Montana. My partner and I hiked and climbed for hours and hours each day, glassed until our eyes popped out and called and called until we were hoarse. No elk. By day six I was pretty worn down—my muscles sore, my feet blistered—and I was suffering from too little sleep. My buddy? He was in as bad of shape as I was, but you'd never know it from talking to him. Every morning his attitude was, "Today's the day!" Then later, over another delicious supper of freeze-dried gruel he'd smile and say, "We'll get 'em tomorrow!" How could I possibly give up with a guy like that around?

So day after day we struck off well before dawn, climbing and listening for a bull to bugle nearby. We'd glass and call, hike to another drainage and do it all over again. We'd pitch off into another black timber hellhole, not worrying about more tears in our clothes or scratches on our faces. In the afternoon we'd take a refreshing catnap, something I find critical in wilderness hunting. Later, we'd stagger back into camp well after dark. We never gave up. Despite the tough hunting and hard work, we were having a pretty good time.

On the morning of day seven, our luck changed. A bull answered my bugle close by, down in a dark timber patch. We knew from passing the area several times before that it held a large wallow. We got the wind right, then attacked, focusing on the wallow. Don moved ahead and set up while I raked a tree and squealed like a small bull feeling his oats. That big 5x5 never hesitated, charging in to whip my behind. The bad news for him was that he charged 23 yards to Don's left. The bull never knew what hit him.

Attitude Is Everything

The key to our success on that tough backpack hunt was as much our attitude as our physical conditioning or hunting skills. We enjoyed each other's company, marveled at some of the most spectacular country found anywhere and worked hard each day, knowing that every step took us closer to our elk and that success was just around the next corner. Packing that meat out was a labor of love.

It can be the same for you. But before you come West elk hunting, or venture up into the mountains if you're a Westerner already, remember that most elk hunts are as much hard, demanding work as anything else. It will likely rain or snow, the wind will blow and the elk will somehow disappear off the face of the earth for long stretches at a time. The mountains will seem to get steeper and steeper each day. More than once you'll fantasize about a hot shower, clean underwear and a hot pizza with everything on it.

But that's all part of what makes elk hunting the wonderful, magical experience that it is. By being mentally prepared for the worst, you'll hunt at your best. When it's all said and done, you'll have wonderful stories to share with your friends for years to come, not negative memories that reflect your dark mood.

Stay sharp mentally: It's not always easy, but it's so important. Leave your troubles and worries in town. They'll be there waiting for you when you get home. Now it's time to hunt, and hunt hard! Don't waste a minute of this wonderful time.

Elk hunting is hard work—full of bad weather, tough country and an animal that can be very hard to find. Only PMA—positive mental attitude—will carry you through the difficult times on the path to success.

Chapter 4

CALLING ALL ELK

The night was a chilly one, with the cloudless sky overflowing with countless stars. My watch read 3:00 a.m. as I reluctantly crawled out of the warmth of my sleeping bag to answer nature's call. I stood just outside my tent and found Orion, a constellation I always search for when hunting. Orion, "the hunter," has always been a sort of good luck charm for me, and I feel better about my chances every time I see him.

There—what was that? I listened intently, wide awake now, for that strange sound. There it was again. It was a bull elk bugling, his deep bass rising to a shrill whistle that seemed to shake the aspen leaves. Soon I heard another bull, then another and another, all answering the challenge in the darkness. I crawled back into my bag but never went back to sleep. Instead, I listened to that primal screaming until the eastern sky began to lighten, when I literally began running to the sound of the nearest bugle, my spirit filled with the joy of wilderness and freedom.

Nothing in North American big-game hunting—not the sight of a majestic Dall sheep ram on a mountain glacier, the thrill of stalking a mountain grizzly on the tundra, a giant muley buck slipping through the sage, the steam coming from the nostrils of a big 10-point whitetail buck in November—excites me the way the sound of a bull elk bugling does. Looking out over the high mountains, the leaves turning from green to gold, grassy meadows glistening with morning dew, bubbling streams steaming with mist ... the primal sound of the bugle makes the hair stand up on the back of my neck like nothing else.

Elk are very vocal animals. But while elk hunters associate elk calling with bugling, there is much more to it than that. Cow and calf sounds are important too, and the excited cow-in-heat call can be deadly when hunters use it in the right place at the right time. This fall, by thinking and moving like an elk and by making the right elk sounds at the right time, you may be fortunate enough to feel the power of a big herd bull as he comes to your calling.

Maybe ...

Basic Elk Sounds

For most of the 20th century, people learned very little about the sounds elk make. Sure, we recognized that elk were vocal animals, but beyond the fact that bulls bugled during the rut and cows barked when alarmed, we were content to leave it at that. Calves? Like good children everywhere, they were seen and not heard, content to learn to bugle and bark but saving the sounds for when they grew up.

In reality, elk are always very vocal animals. Spend much time around elk herds and you'll hear them make all sorts of different sounds. That goes for both sexes and all age classes at all times of the year. You'll hear them talk on the summer range in the tall grasses and high meadows, during the fall breeding season of course, on the winter range in the snow and cold and during the coming of spring.

The basic language of elk is what we commonly call "cow talk." Interestingly, cows are not the only ones using it. Calves do, too. So do bulls. It's a language that can draw in not only elk but other ungulates, too—as well as predators like bears, coyotes and wolves. But let's start with how the calves learn to vocalize, and with what bulls have to say.

Kids at Play

Shortly after calf elk are born—usually in June—they begin to walk and learn about their new world. All the while they hear their family—the elk herd—mewing, squealing and barking around them. Soon they, too, are vocalizing, especially in nursery groups and at play. Just like children, they love to talk and this is apparent as they explore their new world.

This is a period of social involvement for calves, a time when they are actively learning the meaning of vocalizations by adults. This is especially true when danger approaches, a time when a calf learns the value and security of the herd and how to recognize other individual elk—especially its mother—by voice. As summer passes into fall, calves begin mewing and barking just like their mothers, learning that certain sounds are appropriate for certain situations.

A Bunch of Bull

Most elk hunters are concerned with the sounds mature bulls make. The best known of these sounds is, of course, the bugle and the grunting sounds associated with it. However, there are many variations of the basic bugle, and bulls also make many other sounds as well.

The "basic" bugle starts with a deep, low note, rises for several octaves, holds a high-pitched whistling note for a few seconds, then descends back down through the scale. At a distance most bugling sounds like a flute, but the sound can vary greatly. Some bulls sound like they're screaming in pain, some like moaning Hereford bulls, some like they're gargling gravel. No two bulls sound the same.

In addition to the basic bugle, bulls also grunt and chirp and chuckle. I'm not sure how to describe these sounds except to say that when you hear them in the field for the first time, you'll either recognize the sounds as a bull elk or you'll think some demonized banshee is coming to call you home. The best way to learn about these sounds is to purchase one of the inexpensive elk calling cassettes available from game call companies like Knight & Hale, Wilderness Sound Productions,

During the rut, elk hunting is defined by the regal sound of a bull bugling his challenge to the world. Every time I hear it, it makes the hair stand up on the back of my neck.

Lohman Game Calls, Primos and Woods Wise. Listen to the tape and practice your own elk calls at the same time. The time to learn to produce realistic elk sounds is not on opening day but well before the season opens. Practice, practice, practice.

Bulls also "talk" with their antlers during the rut in the form of rubbing and raking them against small trees and brush, and tearing up the ground as they rub the velvet off their racks, then later in mock battle as they prepare to fight other bulls for breeding rights. Raking is a definite form of bull elk communication and should not be overlooked or underestimated by the elk hunter.

Cow talk is the basic language of an elk herd. All elk make these soft mewing sounds, as well as several variations thereof. Because mature cows control the movements of the herd, understanding cow talk is important in understanding how elk interact with each other.

Cow Talk

The most powerful force in contemporary elk calling isn't bugling, grunting, groaning, chuckling or even raking on trees. It's cow calling.

Cow talk is the universal language of elk. The basic sound is a sort of cross between a high-pitched chirp and a mew. The pitch and length of the call varies with the age of the elk and the individual, with younger elk making a higher-pitched, shorter mew and older cows producing a deeper, more drawn-out tone. Bulls make this sound, too, using it all year around.

What does cow talk mean? No one can say for sure except that, as herd animals more comfortable in the company of other elk than alone, cow talk communicates an elk's presence to others. Perhaps in the summer calving season, when elk are more concerned with herd behavior than at other times, they try to keep track of each other. During the pre-rut, it might advertise a cow's willingness to join a harem of other cows. During the rut, variations of the basic mew definitely advertise a cow's readiness to breed. At all times of the year it seems to be a sound that tells all other elk within earshot that, *hey, everything's all right over here, why not come see me?*

The other basic sound a cow makes is the alarm bark. The bark has a deep resonating tone that sounds amazingly like a dog's bark. It means one thing—danger! When a cow barks loudly, it is a sign for all elk within earshot to run for their lives.

We still have much to learn about the sounds elk make and why they make them. Can individual elk recognize other individual elk by the pitch and tone of their voices? I believe they can. That's one reason, I believe, that too much bugling will shut the elk up for miles. They have already heard the local bulls bugling for days, weeks and, in some cases, years. They know what the others sound like. *Who is this new bugler on the block? Things don't seem right!* I firmly believe that herd bulls and, more importantly, old herd cows, identify unfamiliar bugling as a threat to the security of their herd simply because it represents an unknown.

Basic Elk Calls

There are several different types of elk calls, all of which have a place in the modern elk hunter's arsenal. These include (top row, left to right) the Lohman Bugler reed call, Knight & Hale Challenger external diaphragm call, Knight & Hale Extend-A-Tone Elk Bugler, and Lohman World Record Elk Call; and (center row, left to right) Lohman Elk Talker cow call, Knight & Hale Magnum Cow Estrus cow call, and Lohman Screamin' Hot Cow call. Internal diaphragm calls (bottom row) are the most versatile elk calls of all. You can make both bull and cow sounds with them.

I went on my very first elk hunt in the late 1970s in mid-September, horsebacking 20 miles into Idaho's Selway Wilderness Area with a salty old outfitter who lived in western Montana. He showed me the magic of calling elk. That old-timer didn't need any fancy store-bought calls—there really weren't a lot of good ones around then anyway—but instead bugled with his own voice. How he did that I'll never know. I tried to get it down for years, but all I got out of it was a very sore throat, sounding more like I was pitifully drowning than like a stoked-up bull elk ready to fight.

Some hunters can call elk with their voices, but most of us can't. That's okay. Today there are so many excellent commercial elk calls available at reasonable prices that learning to make realistic elk sounds isn't all that difficult.

Diaphragm Calls

The most versatile elk call of all is the simple internal latex diaphragm call. Diaphragms were first used to imitate turkey sounds. Then, back in the early 1970s, someone figured out that they could make realistic bugling sounds using this same diaphragm call. A revolution in elk calling was just beginning.

With diaphragm calls, you can make virtually every sound elk make—including bull, cow and calf sounds. The diminutive diaphragm fits completely inside your mouth, so you can use it without making any hand movements—a big advantage especially when bowhunting but when rifle hunting as well.

However, diaphragms do have their shortcomings. First, they're very fragile and easy to tear and will eventually wear out, so you always want to carry some spares. And some people—those with a high palate, like me, or those missing some teeth—have trouble using them properly. Many hunters combine a diaphragm with a grunt tube, which helps produce a deeper resonating tone when bugling.

There are some external diaphragm calls available—like the Imitator from Wilderness Sound Productions—that stretch the diaphragm over the end of a plastic tube. You regulate the sounds by changing your lip pressure on the latex as you blow. I've used this call for years, and it works very well.

Reed Calls

A reed bugle call features a metal reed housed inside a mouthpiece that's connected to a grunt tube. Reed calls are easy to blow but can only be used at maximum volume, making them useless at close range. They can be as effective as long-range locator calls, but their effectiveness ends there.

However, external reed-type cow calls have proven themselves very effective. With them, you can make both the basic mews and chirps as well as one of the most exciting new calling techniques in elk hunting: the excited cow-in-heat call. Some reed-type cow calls have an exposed reed and some a covered reed, while you control others' pitch and tone by biting down on the mouthpiece. Excellent calls of this type include the Knight & Hale Real Cow Talker and Magnum Estrus Cow, Sceery Special Cow Elk Call, Woods Wise Hyper-Hot Cow Call, Carlton's Fight'n Cow and Lonesome Cow, Lohman Cow Talker and Primos Lead Cow & Calf Call.

Calling Kits

One of the best ways to get started calling elk is to purchase a kit complete with elk calls, a cassette tape and a video all in one package. The Knight & Hale Elk Calling Kit, Lohman Deluxe Elk Calling Kit, Primos Trophy Bull Elk Calling Kit, Carlton's Call Elk Calling Kit, E.L.K. Inc. Calling System and Sceery Trophy Bull Elk Kit all include easy-to-use elk calls along with all the instructional materials you'll need to get started.

I sure wish these teaching aids had been available when I first started learning to make elk sounds. Maybe then I wouldn't have wrecked my throat trying to learn that voice-bugling stuff!

Choosing an Elk Call

Virtually all internal diaphragm calls are the same, regardless of whose name is stamped on the package. Reed-type calls are different, though, and each has a slightly different tone and feels a bit different to use. Here, you may want to try a couple of different calls out before you decide which one to take hunting.

When I go elk hunting today, I usually have several different types of elk calls in my daypack. I believe that making the same exact sounds, day in and day out, is a sure way to turn the elk off. Often, just changing the pitch and tone of your calling by simply switching to a different brand or type of call is all you need to do to get elk fired up again. Also, when working a bull, I'll often use two or three different calls at the same time, trying to make him think there is more than one elk where I am. I think that gives him confidence that the noises he hears from down the way really are more elk and not some dude from the coffee shop trying to turn him into hamburger.

Basic Calling Strategies

Like all forms of big-game hunting, the strategies and techniques of calling elk have evolved quite a bit over the past few decades. From using primitive whistles as bugles to today's more sophisticated calls and techniques, the discipline continues to evolve.

The most exciting development in elk calling in recent years is the emphasis on cow talk—rather than bugling—as hunters' primary tool.

Is Bugling Ancient History?

Today's bulls have grown up around elk hunters. They've all heard more than their share of imitation bugling and know that it means danger; too many hunters have blown too many bugles—both during the season and during preseason scouting sessions. Many experienced elk hunters believe most of those bulls that crazily charged right in to the bugle have been killed, their careless genes erased from the gene pool. Those cautious bulls that refused to come in are the ones left alive, passing that cautious genetic trait on to future generations.

No one can prove whether or not there is any truth to that. What you can prove to yourself by lots of elk hunting is that mature bulls, and especially those on public lands, rarely come to the bugle with reckless abandon like they used to. In fact, when elk hear your bugling they'll often just shut up. Often you'll hear them bugling only at night.

But that doesn't mean bugling is ancient history. It just means you have to be judicious in your bugle use. Today, I use the bugle primarily as a locator call, hoping to get a response, then moving in as close as I can to where I think the bull is located before trying either to slip in undetected or lure him in with cow talk. Not that mature bulls won't come to a bugle; they certainly will. It's just that everything has to be just right before they'll make that commitment.

The one elk that will still charge in to the bugle is the young satellite bull. These two- to four-year-old "raghorns" are bulls that orbit harems gathered up by herd bulls, hoping to slip in and do some breeding when big daddy isn't watching. Their testosterone levels are out of control, and they can't wait to fight any other bull around—i.e., you—so they might get a little breeding action in here too.

While bugling is still part of an elk hunter's repertoire—both as a locator call and a means of luring in bulls—using cow talk is a much more effective means of luring elk within range. Both basic cow calling and excited cow calling (imitating the sounds of a cow in heat) can be extremely effective.

Creating a Setup

You should never use your elk calls without assuming you'll get a response from a nearby elk that you may not have seen yet, with that bull charging in on you. In reality this rarely happens, but it takes place often enough that if you're not prepared, it can cost you what may have been your only shot opportunity during a tough hunt.

When you set up for a shot while calling elk, there are several things you should always try to do.

Play the Wind

Without the wind in your favor, everything else is moot. Remember that the bull will probably try to swing downwind from you, so always keep a shooting lane open to the downwind side.

Stay Hidden

Never underestimate an elk's eyesight. Use the available brush and trees to create a natural blind that both conceals your presence and breaks up your outline.

Create Shooting Lanes

Never bury yourself into the brush so deeply that you can't get a shot to your left, right and directly out front. Break branches off violently if you have to. An elk often confuses this sound with that of another bull raking a tree. (See inset in diagram at right.)

Use the Terrain

Try to set up so elk do not have to cross tough terrain features like deep ravines or wide creeks. Bulls will often hesitate at these natural barriers, and this hesitation can ruin your chances immediately. I like to set up so the bull has to approach me from downhill. This does two things: First, it makes it easier for me to see him coming; second, it lets gravity work for me, not against me, should I have to pick up and move at the last moment to keep the elk from getting my wind. (See diagram on page 68.)

Stay Flexible

You'll often have to set up several times before you actually get a shot. While patience is a virtue—watch out for those bulls that come in silently!—be prepared to pick up and move, then set up again, if and when the situation dictates.

When creating a setup, it is important to make open lanes in the thick cover through which you can shoot. Don't be shy: Break branches, snap off twigs, be noisy if you have to clear your lanes. Try to make shooting lanes to the front and both sides, making sure you can shoot downwind too, if necessary. Bulls often try to flank you downwind, so having open shooting lanes to the side—that can give you a shot before the elk gets your wind—is critical. Your lanes won't be as obvious as the ones drawn here (see inset) for illustrative purposes, but you get the idea: With all the work you're going through to get a bull in, you'd better be able to take a shot.

Use the Terrain to Set Up

Use the terrain to your advantage, using trees, brush and dips in the terrain for cover, and keep gravity on your side. Here, from atop a timbered ridge (A), the hunters have heard a bull bugle. They smartly get the wind right and move down toward the elk, keeping themselves above the bull (B). When they reach the edge of the brushy lodgepole stand and are faced with semi-open brush and small-diameter peckerpole pines (C), they build a setup and try to get the bull in, forcing him to walk uphill to them, with the wind in their faces.

The Importance of Cow Talk

Here's where cow calling comes in. Because basic cow calls are the universal language of elk, because elk in herds are always talking back and forth and because basic cow chirps and mews are a comforting, nonconfrontational sound, rarely will they spook elk the way a raucous, raspy, challenging bugle can. You can even call back elk that you have shot at with a firearm or hit with an arrow to lure them back in for another shot. A cow call can do it, and it's not fantasy—it's fact. It's worth trying for the time or two when it will work!

There are several ways to use a cow call. Many successful hunters softly blow their cow calls all day long as they hike through the woods. They believe that if they accidentally stumble into an elk herd or if nearby elk hear them walking, the cow talk will reassure those elk that all is well. Another good way to use cow calls is to work the upper edges of timbered pockets, cow calling down into the timber every few hundred yards. And when you're finally in close to the elk herd, judicious cow calling can draw a bull over to round you up.

The basic sequence of using the cow call should be to try to represent calm cow or calf elk. Call like this: Make a single soft, high-pitched call, wait 5 seconds, call again, wait 30 seconds, call again, wait 2 minutes, repeat sequence, wait 1 minute, call again and then wait 20 minutes for a response. When you get a response, you know the elk are close, so try to slip in, set up and use the cow talk to draw a curious or protective bull in to investigate.

The Excited Cow

The excited cow is an interesting variation on cow calling, a technique that has accounted for success in taking an inordinate number of quality bulls. It's a calling sequence that doesn't work all the time—what type of game calling does?—but it has been so effective that you need to incorporate it into your own elk hunting bag of tricks.

During the breeding season, individual cow elk come into estrus at different times. A herd bull will round up as many cows as he can control at one time, working himself into a lather as he tries to control herd movements and attempts to keep other bulls from cutting in on his action and breeding some of his cows as they come into heat. He wants it all for himself and will do whatever it takes to service estrus cows before another bull can slip in and beat him to the punch.

Cows let the bull know they're ready to breed in several ways, body posture and smell being the two most prominent signals. But cows also send the message vocally. As a cow gets closer and closer to being ready to breed, her vocalizations turn from a passive, calm, single- or double-noted mew to an excited, high-pitched sequence of multiple mews and chirps that can drive bulls absolutely wild. Hearing those excited cow sounds, a big bull will often charge right on over in an attempt to keep control over her and, if possible, breed that cow right now.

By slipping in close to an elk herd during breeding season and making these same excited cow sounds, the elk hunter just might draw in a big old bull that he could never call in any other way. Several call companies have capitalized on this phenomenon and developed calls designed to imitate this excited cow calling. They include the Knight & Hale Magnum Cow Estrus, Woods Wise Hyper-Hot, Primos Lead Cow & Calf, Sceery Special Cow Elk and Lohman Cow Talker cow calls.

Stay Flexible

It is very important when trying to call elk that you remain flexible, altering your basic strategies and techniques as the situation dictates. No two calling situations are ever exactly the same. Hunters who have the ability to go with the flow, adapting calling volumes and styles by giving the elk what they want to hear, have the best chances at success.

Late-Season Calling

Everyone knows you can't call elk in after the rut is over, right? Not necessarily ...

One year, I was hunting a special late October muzzleloader-only season in Colorado. It had been a slow first few days when, out of nowhere, I heard a bull vigorously bugle down below me. Soon there were four bulls bugling their heads off. Not having a call in my pocket—elk don't call late after the rut, you know—I instead slipped down off my glassing perch and weaseled my way down through the dark timber, where I managed to shoot a very nice 5x5 who didn't know the rut was over.

In truth, the elk rut isn't over in September, as most suspect. Some elk breed into October and even November. I've heard enough elk bugling during early October rifle seasons that I'll bugle too from time to time, trying to con a bull into giving himself away.

The most effective calling during late season, though, is cow talk. Elk make cow sounds all year round, and you can still draw bulls in with judicious cow talk during gun season. To be sure, calling is much tougher in late season than during the rut, especially in areas where there's a lot of hunting pressure.

Cow calls, calf sounds and bull squeals are the most effective sounds to make at this time. It is important not to overcall. I like to hike through the timber until I find fresh elk sign, then set up and call a couple of times, giving myself plenty of time to get a response before moving on. Bulls who come to late-season cow calling will probably do so silently, so make sure you're well hidden, and stay alert.

When still-hunting silently through the dark timber during gun season, keep your ears open, as well as your eyes. You're most likely to hear elk making cow talk early and late in the day, when they're most active, but during the day they'll get up and stretch, relieve themselves and grab a

snack or drink. At these times they'll often talk to each other. I also always keep my nose open as I still-hunt into the wind. Many times I've smelled elk bedded in the dark timber long before I've seen them. When that happens, I'll get the wind exactly right, move in as close as I dare, then make some very soft cow and calf sounds. On more than one occasion, I've watched a hidden bull elk stand up out of his bed in response to this late-season cow talk.

Chapter 5

The Magic of the Rut

The elk rut is a magical, mysterious time. It's a season of change, when the greens and blues of summer turn into the golds, yellows and oranges of fall; when days grow shorter, nights crisper and the world begins taking on a sharper edge. It's also a time of unpredictability, when sunny mornings can become dark with rain clouds and when calm days can become filled with strong, bone-chilling winds.

It's a time when the high country rings with the sound of bugling bull elk, their eerie wailing echoing across vast canyons as they proudly announce for all to hear that they are the bull of the woods, the master of all they survey. To all challengers they boldly say, "Stay away or be whipped within an inch of your lives!" There is no more wonderful time to be in the mountains of the West than now, during the magic of the elk rut.

For elk hunters, the rut is a time of hope. Confident that bugling bulls will give their locations away, hunters hope that their calling ability, their stalking skills and their expertise in setting an ambush will bear fruit—that one frosty morning the bull of their dreams will make a mistake and come barreling in, presenting that close-range shot that has been dreamed about for the past 11 long months. And if not, maybe the heavens will smile down upon you and let you at least see the bull of the mountain up-close and personal, his dark mane framing a massive set of polished antlers as he comes close, but not quite close enough.

And then, for the next 11 months, you'll dream about him, hoping that next time you'll get your shot. Next time, you promise yourself, things will be different ...

Bowhunting Basics

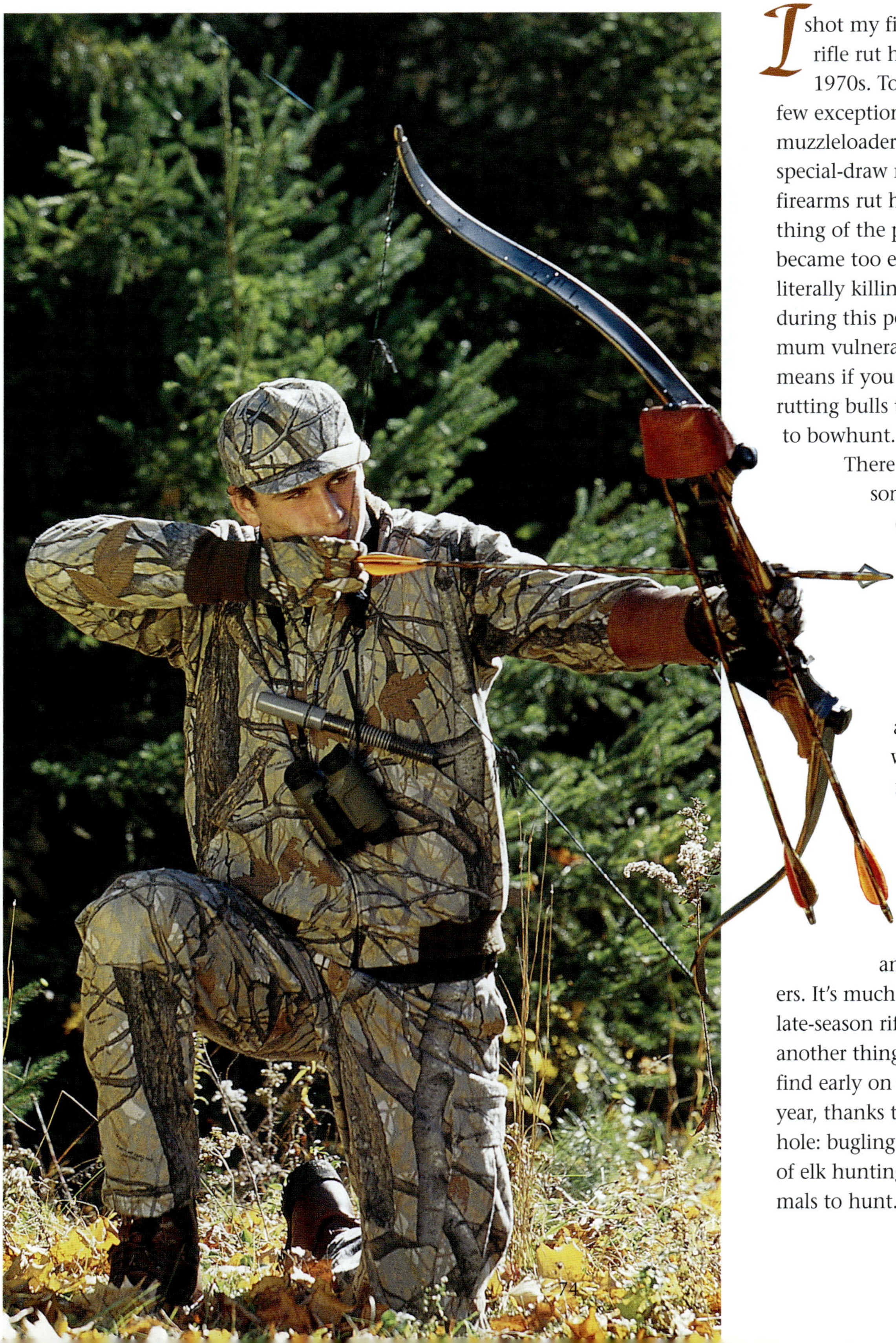

I shot my first bull during a rifle rut hunt in the late 1970s. Today, with very few exceptions—some general muzzleloader hunts and a few special-draw rifle hunts—firearms rut hunts for elk are a thing of the past. Hunters became too effective and were literally killing all the bulls during this period of maximum vulnerability. That means if you want to hunt rutting bulls today you have to bowhunt.

There are several reasons to bowhunt elk during the early archery-only seasons found in every state in the West. For one thing, the days are long and the weather warm, with some rain showers and thunderstorms; the mountain meadows are full of tall lush grasses and colorful flowers. It's much nicer than cold, late-season rifle hunts. For another thing, elk are easier to find early on than later in the year, thanks to your ace in the hole: bugling. The hardest part of elk hunting is finding animals to hunt. But when your quarry yells and screams and thrashes the brush, that makes the game all the easier.

Finally, you can call elk to you during the September rut. This is get-in-their-face, go-get-'em hunting, and nothing is more exciting. The sound of the bugle will make the hair on the back of your neck stand straight up and get your heart trying to pound its way right out of your chest. The first time you call 800 pounds of raging bull into your lap, his bloodshot eyes bugged out, his dark chocolate mane dripping with sweat, his strong-smelling glands overpowering your nostrils, you'll wonder what in the world you've gotten yourself into.

Bowhunters are always better served setting up in thickets rather than open terrain. This country is more conducive to a bull coming in close enough for a shot before he gets suspicious. Make sure you have open shooting lanes and try to force the bull to come uphill to you.

When to Hunt

As with deer, the elk rut can be divided into three basic periods—pre-rut, peak of the rut and post-rut. Most early bow seasons overlap the pre-rut and peak of the rut, so the question becomes, "Which is the best time to hunt?"

There's no wrong answer. During the peak of the rut, which occurs in most areas roughly during the last three weeks of September, there will be more cows in heat and therefore more frenzied activity on the parts of bulls of all sizes and age classes. You'll probably hear more bugling during this time. The downside is the fact that as the rut peaks, the bulls have already established their pecking order around harems of cows. The herd bulls spend most of their time protecting their harems, circling the cows endlessly as they ward off interloping satellite bulls, or rounding them up and herding them away from the challenges of other bugling bulls—and bugling bowhunters. Even though you can hear lots of screaming and can often make a herd bull go absolutely wild with your calling, it can be tough to bugle a bull in during the rut's peak.

For the most part bulls are still establishing their pecking order and rounding up harems during the pre-rut, which generally occurs from early August until early September. They're very active, and their anxiety levels are high. They're more apt to come to skillful calling now simply because their hormones are overpowering their natural inclination toward caution. You may not hear as many bulls bugling as you would a few weeks later, but the ones you do hear are often easier (a relative term) to call in.

Locating a Bull

We'll cover locating elk more thoroughly in the next section; however, it is important to remember that the key in successful early-season bowhunting is finding a bull to hunt. Because elk are herd animals that live in small pockets of their available range at any one time, you need to cover some ground. When foot hunting, I am always prepared to cover anywhere between 5 to 15 miles a day searching for elk.

Once you locate a bull, it's time to move in close and get to work fast!

Setting Up

We covered the basic setup in the "Basic Calling Strategies" section of chapter four. For bowhunters, we'll take setup a bit further.

You're always better off setting up in thick stuff than on open hillsides or ridges. Why? Because when an elk comes to your calling, he will both know exactly where you are and be suspicious if he doesn't see another elk when he gets close. If bulls can see from a significant distance that there are no other elk in the area they're viewing, they often stop and look intently for the other elk and, when they don't see any, simply drift away. I like to set up in thick brush or lodgepole pines or along small meadow edges where I can shoot 20 to 35 yards without fear of my arrow being deflected.

You need something to break up your outline. I like to set up with my back against a tree trunk, à la turkey hunting, with brush or small evergreen trees around me. This gives me a chance to maneuver and get the shot without being obstructed, yet not stand out like a sore thumb. Of course, you need to be totally camouflaged, but it's just as important that you do not move. Sharp-eyed elk will spot the slightest movement and be gone in a flash. I like to set up on my knees, and I have practiced shooting from both knees enough that I can consistently make this type of shot. Sometimes I'll set up standing, hidden behind a tree trunk or, more ideally, in the center of a small cluster of three or four small-diameter trees that allow me to shoot to both sides as well as out front.

It's always best if you can get the bull to come uphill to you. It's easier for you to see him coming that way, and he'll generally be moving more slowly than if he were charging you down the slope. Also, if you have to move and get set up again, it's much easier to do so running downhill than against the forces of gravity.

Be ready for the bull to try to come in on the downwind side of your setup. Ideally, you'll have open shooting lanes to either side that present opportunities before the bull intersects the path of your scent; that's where you'll often get your shot. Be prepared to release an arrow quickly, if an opportunity avails itself, if the bull gets past these lanes and closes in on being truly "downwind."

Stick & Move

Here's the ideal scenario: You locate your bull, move in, get set up, call him right to you and end up with a picture-perfect, under-30-yard broadside shot. And it does happen that way. Once in a blue moon. More likely though, you'll play a stick-&-move game with your bull as he moves on a path you hadn't anticipated, the wind changes direction slightly or he doesn't come at all.

Most important is the wind. Do whatever it takes—run as fast as you can, sounding like a Sherman tank if you must—to keep the wind in your favor. One whiff of your body odor, and it's all over; that elk is *gone*. Try to stay hidden as you move, of course, using available terrain and brush as your cover.

If the bull hangs up, try to creep in closer. At all times, be alert for other elk or the bull suddenly coming to you silently. Find another good-looking place, set up and try calling him to you again. Or, if you can, slip in and simply shoot him. The last three bulls I've taken with my bow have all been shot after I slipped in on them unaware, getting the shot as they were raking a tree.

When a bull decides to leave, taking his cows away from you, you have two choices—give up or go get him. I've had virtually no success trying to follow elk through the woods. Occasionally I have had success circling them, moving as quickly as I can, getting in front of their

Stick-&-Move Strategy

Rarely does a bull come charging right in, like the textbooks say he will. Usually you'll have to play it fast and loose, countering the different moves the elk will make as he tries to get downwind of you. Remember: Do whatever it takes to keep the wind right. Run and make enough noise to wake the dead if you must. Here as hunter and bull elk move toward each other (A), the bull tries to flank the hunter and get downwind (B). As the elk slides with the breeze and tries to circle downwind (C), so does the hunter until they end up close enough for the hunter to shoot (D).

Bowhunters must remain flexible in their approach as they move in on an elk herd to try to get a shot. The most important thing? Keep the wind in your favor.

anticipated line of march, then setting up and letting them come to me.

Often you'll have to make a circle of a mile or more as you stay above their position. As you go, try to keep track of their movements by listening for the bull to bugle, chuckle or rake a tree; also listen for cow talk or the sound of the herd walking. Sometimes you have to rely solely on your ability to read the mountain (knowing they're heading for a bedding area) and blind luck. Once you're ahead of the elk, slip down the slope and set up. If you can get set up and have the elk march past you, you have an excellent chance for a shot at a calm bull. Remember that the herd bull is usually last in line. If he moves past your hiding spot, cow calling can sometimes bring him into position for a shot. Or, if you can get between the herd bull and his harem, squealing like an immature satellite bull and following with a couple of cow calls and some raking, you just might send that big bull into a rage. He will think a small bull has sneaked into his harem and is trying to steal one of his prized cows. Nothing makes him any madder—or less cautious.

One thing's for certain—the more you bowhunt rutting elk, the more you realize there are no hard-and-fast rules, no easy paths to success. It's always hard work, and it takes a generous dose of luck to get a quality shot. Regardless, there are few hunting challenges more thrilling—or more addictive—than bowhunting rutting bulls. Try it sometime, and you'll see what I mean.

Often you'll have to play a "stick-&-move" game with a bull to get a shot. Rarely will the elk come right in to you. Often he'll circle downwind or herd up his cows and move off. When that happens, try to circle the herd, getting in front of its anticipated line of march, and set up an ambush.

Locating a Bull to Hunt

When hunting elk, the most difficult part of the equation is often simply locating a bull to hunt. To that end, be prepared to spend the vast majority of your hunt searching for pockets of elk.

It's pretty basic, but many hunters forget this important fact: You can't shoot 'em if you can't find 'em. Even in the very best elk country, locating a bull to hunt can be time consuming and downright frustrating. Here's how to go about it.

The basic scenario goes something like this. I grudgingly crawl out of my warm sleeping bag well before daylight and hike in the dark to a vantage point that allows me to glass open pockets and meadows while also listening for bulls bugling. Sometimes I get up by 3:00 a.m. to listen, as bulls often bugle wildly at night then taper off after the sun's up. If I hear a bull just before or just after daylight, the plan is simple—attack! If not, it's time to get the lead out.

I now move rapidly through the country, often bugling or cow calling as I go, hoping to hear a bull to hunt. There's no need to waste any time sneaking—you need to cover maximum ground during the "prime time" of the morning's first few hours. Use your topo maps to guide you, working bench areas where elk might bed, dark timber pockets, timber stringers leading from feeding meadows to likely bedding areas and so forth.

A fresh rub still dripping sap is a sign that there's a bull somewhere close by. This would be a good place to try to locate a bull with your calls.

Hot Sign? Cool Your Heels

When you come to an area with hot sign—fresh tracks, droppings or worked-over wallows—slow down and look and listen for elk. I've heard them walking or cow talking and have often heard the sound of a bull raking his antlers on a nearby tree. Try some calling yourself. Your goal is to get a bull to sound off. Always be ready, especially when you call. You never know when a bull will come charging in. I've had enough elk bust me when I wasn't ready that I never, ever call without hiding myself first. Be sure to give yourself some time in hot-sign areas. It may take a bull 20 or 30 minutes to answer your calling. And he may come in silently.

Early one morning in southwestern Montana, I was moving through some lodgepole stringers when I came upon a freshly used wallow that was peppered with fresh tracks and steamy droppings. Obviously, elk had passed through not long before, so I sat and listened. Nothing. I bugled, softly at first, using grunts and chuckles as the primary sounds. Nothing. Cow calls. Nothing. A loud bugle. Nothing. After 20 minutes I was getting ready to move on when I thought I heard something. The wind made it tough to hear, but there it was—the sound of a bull elk raking a tree. He had to be close! I went into stealth mode, slowly working toward that sound. Reaching a small brushy mound, I carefully peeked through the brush to see a big, dark-horned 5x5 bull destroying a small pine not 50 yards away across a shallow ravine. While he was venting his frustrations, I belly-crawled through the brush to within 30 yards. I'm still wondering how I shot over his back.

Another time, my friend Merritt Pride and I were working a timbered ridge when we got a violent response to our calling. We set up and got into a tempo with that bull, when all of a sudden it got deathly quiet. We waited ... and waited ...

Bull elk love to wallow in the mud during the rut, often crusting themselves over with gunk. When you locate a freshly used wallow, you know there's a bull in the area.

and waited. After 15 minutes I told Merritt I was going to move up and see if I could find that bull. I hadn't taken two steps when Merritt hissed at me. Freezing, I peeked up under the brim of my hat to see a very good 6x6 bull staring me in the face, not 35 yards away. He came in as silently as the proverbial church mouse. I chanted to myself, "I'm a bush, I'm a bush!" It didn't work. He was out of there like a shot.

The lesson is this: Bulls don't always respond with loud, aggressive bugling. You have to be ready for anything.

You Don't Have to Call

Don't overlook glassing or taking a stand in the dark timber itself when trying to locate bulls to hunt.

Glassing up elk as they move from feeding areas to their beds early in the day is a great way to locate elk, especially at long distances from your spot. At the same time, you can be listening for bugling and other elk sounds. Once you find the elk, you can figure out how to hunt them.

If you don't glass up any elk or don't hear them calling, does that mean the area is devoid of animals? Certainly not. Put on your hiking shoes and cover ground. In hot weather, I've enjoyed success by finding a waterhole or wallow peppered with fresh sign, then setting up a portable treestand or building a ground blind on the downwind side, then sitting there from midday until dark. One hot September week in the Gila unit of New Mexico I set just such a stand over a water tank and climbed in under the noonday sun. It was probably 75 or 80°F, but I had a good paperback with me and settled in for a long sit. That evening I saw a black bear (with two game department tags in his ears), a pair of foxes, six mule deer does—and eight elk, six of them cows, one a raghorn and one a small 6x6 bull. I was hunting for a dandy bull and passed him by. But I thought to myself, here's my backup plan just in case I can't get in on a granddaddy.

It's also important to hunt all day. Sure, I nap in the afternoon, but I've had enough bulls answer my calling and watched enough elk come to waterholes or wallows while sitting on stand during the so-called dead period between 10:00 a.m. and 3:00 p.m. that I hunt as hard as I can all day long.

Be flexible. And never, ever give up.

When you locate red-hot elk sign like this tracked-up wallow, slow down! The elk are probably close by. Now's the time to thoroughly work the area over, using all your senses—including your nose and ears—as you try to pin the herd down.

The Moment of Truth

It's all come together, and there he is—a big bull elk, walking defiantly into bow range. All the time, work and sweat comes down to this moment. Can you make the shot?

Patience! The bull may be walking straight toward you. There will probably be lots of brush and tree trunks guarding his body. His eyes are roaming, looking for another elk. He's within rock-throwing distance, but you're far from getting your shot. Now's when you have to overcome "bull fever" and be patient enough to wait for the right moment to draw and shoot.

The only acceptable bow shot at an elk is a broadside or slightly quartering-away angle, which allows the broadhead an unobstructed path to the heart and lung area. Ideally you'll be able to shoot through both lungs. I've seen bulls hit through only one lung travel a long way, making recovery difficult. Hit through both lungs, most elk go down within 100 yards.

When the bull approaches at the wrong angle, stay motionless and silent and wait him out. You have your cleared shooting lanes set up, and the odds are good he'll pass through one of them at the right angle. Wait to draw your bow until the bull's head goes behind a tree or bush so he can't see the movement. You'll really appreciate having a bow with 65 percent to 80 percent let-off set at a draw weight you can easily hold for an extended period of time when you draw on a bull and he stops behind a bush, his head and eyes exposed as he looks for you.

If the bull is walking broadside as he enters an opening you can shoot through, it's best to stop him before releasing the arrow. To do this, use your mouth diaphragm call and make a soft cow mew or low-volume grunt. When you do this, be ready to shoot! When he hears your call he will likely swivel his head to look at you, so as soon as he stops, pick a spot—halfway up the body, 3 to 5 inches behind the front leg bone will center up both lungs—settle your sight pin and release.

After the shot, stay still. Sometimes I like to make some soft cow sounds, both if I hit the bull, or—it happens—if I miss. More than once I've seen bulls shot through both lungs start to bolt, then stop in their tracks when I cow-called to them. After hesitating for a few seconds, they start to walk off until they simply run out of gas and collapse within sight. After a miss, more than one bull has come back to see what the heck is going on. They're much harder to get a shot at now, but it has happened. The key is that they never see you move.

Once the elk is out of sight, stay down and collect yourself. I don't care how many times you've gone through it, you'll be shaking like a leaf. If you're hunting with a buddy, don't talk. The elk might still be close, and you don't want to spook him. Listen for the sound of him running off and for the sound of him crashing to the ground. Visually mark the last spot you saw him with your eyes. After 15 minutes or so, go try to find your arrow, locate his tracks and look for blood. Whatever you do, give him time. The last thing you want to do is push an arrowed, bedded bull

Patience—and overcoming "bull fever" during the moment of truth—will make your shot a success. Wait 30 minutes to an hour before following up.

any further, because he can go for miles. I like to wait at least 30 minutes, and usually an hour, before I start the tracking process. I start the stopwatch on my wristwatch, which lets me know exactly how long it's been no matter how much I'm shaking or how fast the adrenaline is racing.

How close should the shot be? All bowhunters have their own maximum personal shooting distance, and they should always keep their shots within that range. The farthest I ever shot a bull elk is a paced-off 50 steps, but I had a wide-open shooting lane and was able to use my laser range finder on the broadside bull before releasing.

But in general, you'll have your best chances at calling a bull into range in the kind of thick cover that lends itself to short shots of 10 to 30 yards. I personally don't like to let elk get closer than 20 yards from me. It seems like their radar picks me up when they get closer, so my own personal rule of thumb is to take the first good broadside shot I can get at 20 to 30 yards. When setting up, always try to take several range finder readings off tree trunks or thick bushes near where you think the bull might walk. Then when he appears, you'll know exactly how far away he is when he nears a landmark.

When They Won't Come

Just when you think you've got it all figured out, when you think you're one smart elk hunter, fate has a way of slapping you right in the kisser with a large dose of humility. Just as often as bulls can be called into range, as frequently as they can be ambushed from the ground and the trees, they just as often don't cooperate. About the time you think you have them eating out of your hand, they'll bust you and you'll never see or hear them again.

Outsmarting The Herd Bull

There are more problems than you can shake a stick at when trying to get a rutting bull into bow range. Perhaps the biggest problem of all is the herd bull, he of the huge antlers and monstrous body and the dreams of all elk hunters. Most often, the herd bull is a lover, not a fighter. That is: When he hears your challenging bugling, he'll more than likely take his harem and head the

other direction. After all, he's got his harem. Why should he risk losing them in a fight when all he has to do is skedaddle?

You have several options. Earlier, we talked about circling the herd and trying to set up in front of them. Some hunters in top shape will dog the herd, continuing to harass the bull by bugling and raking, hoping he'll finally get tired of the hassle and turn to whip their behinds out of spite. One of my favorite techniques is using the excited cow call, as described earlier in chapter four, "Basic Calling Strategies." You have to slip in relatively close to the herd to make this work, but it can drive a bull elk absolutely nuts to the point that he'll charge over to you, ready to breed. You'd best be ready to shoot!

My favorite way to get a shot at a herd bull, though, is to stalk him silently. A bull like this will often bugle, grunt and groan frequently, making it easy to keep track of where he is. Your hunting partner—if you have one—can continue calling to keep the bull talking while you take off in hot pursuit. I'll circle to get the wind right, trying to get uphill from the bull if I can, before making my move. The problem, of course, comes with the harem itself. There are usually several very alert cows with this bull, so slipping in past their keen noses, radar ears and x-ray vision is extremely difficult.

You have to move slowly and deliberately, and be prepared to hole up for long periods of time if and when the cows get in the way, before making your final move.

Ambushing Elk

Unless they're really spooked by hunters, elk herds will often travel the same general route each day from bed to water to food and back again. You can use this knowledge to your advantage by setting up an ambush.

Say you've glassed elk as they're traveling back to bed in the evening or as they filter down through the timber from beds to food in the evening. During a midday lull in the action, walk over there and check it out. Maybe there's a big trail they're obviously using to travel on. Maybe there's a hidden spring, seep, wallow or mineral lick they're using regularly and lollygagging around at. They may be funneling through a small saddle. Whatever it is, staging an ambush along this known travel route can pay big dividends.

Portable treestands can be great for this, especially when set over wallows or water holes. Building a ground blind also works well. Just make sure you set your blind with the wind foremost in

Charge Him? Yes!

One last point on stalking bull elk: When an elk rakes a tree, his eyes are closed and the sounds he makes obscure his hearing. He is as vulnerable now as he'll ever be. If you can creep to just outside bow range and catch the bull raking, don't hesitate—charge him! Take a range finder reading off a predetermined point this side of the bull, crouch low and run right at him, preferably from a rear quartering angle. When you reach your spot, don't hesitate—shoot him. I've done this on more than one occasion. Who cares if cows are streaming back past you down the slope? As long as you don't push them past the bull, causing him to raise his head and find you, you're golden.

Key Ambush Locations

Sometimes elk just don't come to your calling, but you've either seen them slip through the timber or found some "hot" sign during your hunt. Setting an ambush can be your best bet for success. Good ambush locations include saddles passing over a ridgeline from thick bedding areas to feeding areas (A); a well-used game trail heading from a bedding thicket to lower-elevation grassy meadows (B); a well-used creek crossing through the dark timber, with meadows nearby (C); a timbered finger joining two large meadows that elk might use to travel between the meadows (D); and a freshly used wallow, especially one surrounded with large bull tracks and freshly rubbed trees nearby (E).

your mind (it must be blowing toward you from where you expect the elk), and don't forget about creating open shooting lanes. As with any big-game hunting, whether you're up a tree or not, take special care to hide your outline and not silhouette yourself from your ambush spot.

Decoys

For years and years elk hunters knew what the problem was; they just didn't have the solution. When an elk comes to a call, he's looking for another elk. If he doesn't see one, he'll get nervous and slip off.

The answer: a decoy! But there weren't any. However, one day as I was hunting along, I found the shed from a nice five-point bull. I like sheds, so I packed it back to the tent. The next day I got into a bugling match with one of those bulls that came in to 75 yards, stopped and, not seeing another bull, left. The light bulb went on. The following morning I left camp early, slipping right down into the hole where I'd heard the bull the previous day. Like clockwork he sounded off, and before long I could see him raking a tree 75 yards away, but he was across a deep ravine with no cover. Sneaking further was out of the question.

I nocked an arrow, rested my bow against a stump and started screaming with my bugle, violently shaking the small evergreen tree I had hidden behind. When that bull lifted his head and looked my way, he saw the shaking tree—and that five-point shed sticking above it, waving back and forth. He snapped. It was all I could do to drop the shed, grab my bow and get ready before he crossed that ravine at a trot. I shot him at 5 yards as he stomped past.

Today there are commercial elk decoys available—most notably those by Mel Dutton Decoys and Feather-Flex—that are portable enough to be used in many elk hunting situations. And they do work reasonably well. I sometimes carry the antlers from a McKenzie 3-D elk target with me and use them as described above. They're lightweight and are easy to pack around the woods.

When bulls won't come to your calls, you have to go to plan B. That usually means either silently stalking them or setting an ambush to intercept the moving herd.

Hang Loose

The point of my story is simply this: When elk hunting, go at it with determination and hang loose. Very seldom do things go as the textbook (even this book!) says they should. The elk hunter who is willing to improvise—going with the flow and doing whatever it takes—is the one most likely to get a shot at a rutting bull.

And success is never sweeter.

Chapter 6

The General Rifle Season

It's *finally* here: Opening morning. Couldn't sleep much last night, could you? Can't say I blame you. I never can, either. After a year of waiting, it's time to go elk hunting again, rifle in hand ... what a great feeling!

The general season is when the vast majority of elk hunters take to the mountains. In the most popular and easily accessible areas, hunters will not be alone. In remote backcountry pockets, the chances for solitude—and success—increase.

Regardless of where your camp is, the dreams are the same. Maybe you'll find that big old six-point bull, in all his glory, pacing below your stand as the dawn comes. Perhaps this year the snow will come early, driving the elk down out of the high country where you can sort through them for a good bull. There's a saddle you found last year, and the deep game trail down its center has been nagging you since last December; if you set up here opening morning, will all those other hunters unknowingly push some elk right past you as they head for the safety of the dark timber in the deep gorge below?

Success rates during the general elk seasons are never high, with fewer than a quarter of all elk hunters carrying tags fortunate enough to place one on an elk. You know this. And yet, there's something about elk hunting this time of year. The mountains, the forests and the streams and rivers draw you like a magnet. The camaraderie of hunting camp, of working together with good friends as a team and sharing the bounty of the harvest when it's all over ... how do you explain how important it all is to someone who's never been there?

It's another elk season, filled with hopes and dreams and wonder. This year, your son or daughter may be with you for the first time, their youthful exuberance infectious, their mere presence making the moment even more special. Will they catch the fever, as you have?

How could they not ...

Post-Rut Blues

Most general firearms elk seasons do not open until the rut is, for all intents and purposes, over. The elk may still talk and the occasional bull may bugle. But where the mountains rang with raucous elk bugling just a few weeks earlier, now all that can be heard are tumbling streams and screaming mountain jays.

The general rifle season hunter needs a different game plan from the rut hunter. I can sum that plan up in one word: legwork.

Scout as You Go

As we've seen, elk are herd animals that live in small, isolated pockets in a vast sea of good-looking habitat. A large elk drainage may encompass 100 square miles, but elk may only be living in a handful of places in that entire drainage. To kill a bull, you first have to find one. And you can't find one unless you cover some country.

Our hypothetical 100-square-mile drainage may be 20 miles long and 5

miles wide. It may also encompass a lot of country between the valley floor and the tallest peaks several thousand feet higher. At first, the task seems impossible. How do you hunt this entire place in a week?

The answer is, you don't. You scout on-the-go, splitting up the drainage with your hunting partners. Your first goal isn't necessarily to kill an elk, but to find elk to hunt. Three or four hunters—who are in decent physical shape, know how to climb high and glass early and late, then are able to walk 5 to 10 miles during midday searching for elk sign—can cover the entire drainage in two or three days. This is no time for silent, whitetail-woods still-hunting!

As you move, look for feeding elk in small openings in the timber, elk walking through the semi-open timber on the opposite side of the hill from you and for fresh tracks, trails, beds, droppings and wallows on your side. Keep your ears and nose alert, too, for the sound and smell of elk. Once you find them, it's time to get your buddies and map out a plan to get in on the elk.

Herd Bulls

After rutting, bull elk—especially the old herd bulls—are tired and worn out. They've expended huge amounts of energy breeding and protecting their harems from interloping satellite bulls, often losing a quarter of their body weight. Your scouting efforts may produce lots of elk, but they will more than likely be cows, calves and small- to medium-sized bulls.

Once the rut is over, herd bulls are ready to resume their life of bachelorhood. They often find isolated pockets of deep cover where they can rest without being disturbed by anybody or anything, including other elk. This they do alone or in small groups of other bulls.

You can find these pockets in the dark timber, among blow-downs and other hellhole cover; on small benches notched into the sides of steep, brushy ridges; near high-mountain saddles; on thick creek- and riverbottoms; and in other nasty, inhospitable places. We'll devote an entire chapter to hunting the dark timber a bit later.

Bull elk have a habit of disappearing immediately following the rut. During this time hunters need to look for them high and low, concentrating on covering lots of country and glassing long and hard in search of reclusive bulls.

Plan Carefully

Once you've found the elk, you must plan carefully before making your move. If you spook them with your scent, careless walking and talking or poor shooting, chances are they'll move several miles and you'll have to start all over again.

When approaching the elk, make sure all hunters have cover to hide behind as they move in. Never underestimate an elk's eyesight, especially its ability to spot a careless hunter out in the open with the sun shining on him. Try to move in from either the same elevation as the elk or, ideally, a bit above them. If you're trying a drive—and small drives can work well, especially if you've scouted the area and found places that make natural funnels for escaping elk—place the standers to cover these escape routes and, if you have enough people, a stander to cover any back-door escapees. The drivers should actually still-hunt, doing their best to slip up on the herd, pick out a bull and get a shot before he ever knows what hit him.

Remember, too, that while elk like to bed in the same general area day after day, they won't necessarily bed in exactly the same place day in and day out. So, before moving in on them it is always better to try to spot them first with your optics.

Shot Placement—With Firearms and Archery Gear

Elk are big and strong, with heavy hides and big bones. They are also very tenacious of life—as hard to harvest cleanly as any big-game animal in North America. Shot placement is critical.

When broadside, placing a bullet or arrow just behind the front shoulder—between an area one-third of the way up from the belly line up to one-third of the way below the top of the shoulder—will take out both lungs, your number-one objective. With large calibers shooting heavy bullets, shooting right through the scapula bone is feasible; this could well break the animal's shoulder and anchor it in its tracks. The same is true if the animal is quartering away slightly, except that with a rifle you're trying to break the off-side shoulder while destroying the lungs; with a bow you have to imagine the arrow penetrating through to that far shoulder.

The above described are the only acceptable archery shots.

With a rifle, if the animal is facing you directly, placing the bullet at the base of the throat and/or the sternum will take out the heart and/or lungs as well. However, this shot should be attempted only with heavy calibers and stout bullets. No archery shots.

If the animal is facing away from you, placing the bullet at the base of the tail will break the spine. Again, only stout bullets fired from heavy calibers by skilled marksmen should be used under this condition. But there's a lot of room for error. Best bet? Wait for a better shot—in respect for the animal and in consideration of the hurt and waste you could inflict.

Because an elk has lots of muscle in relation to the size of the spine and trachea, I personally shy away from neck shots with rifle, muzzleloader and archery gear.

Always keep in mind that a poor hit on a big elk can be your worst nightmare. As often as not, poorly hit animals will take you on a tracking job that can cover several miles over rough terrain. When in doubt, wait. Shoot only when the animal is in a good position with no obstructions between you and the elk. Then take your time to ensure a well-placed first shot—with rifle, muzzleloader or archery gear.

Study the photos at right to get an even better idea of proper shot placement on elk.

Broadside

A broadside shot is the perfect opportunity for firearms (rifle and muzzleloader) and archery hunters. Place your projectile halfway up the chest, just a few inches behind the front shoulder (R&B). If your rifle caliber and bullet are big enough, you could try to break through the scapula and anchor him on the spot (R).

Quartering Away

A quartering-away shot is ideal both for firearms hunters and archers. Aim halfway up the chest and try to place your projectile through the chest cavity to the off-shoulder (R&B).

Straight On

There is no bow shot here. With a large-caliber rifle, if you can place the bullet in the center of the dark hair at the base of the throat, you'll take him cleanly (R).

Quartering Toward

Quartering-toward shots can be made with a large-caliber rifle and stout bullets by shooting this bull through the front third of the on-side shoulder, halfway up the body (R). The bullet should smash through that shoulder and into the elk's boiler room. Never attempt this shot with a bow!

Straight Away

With a heavy caliber rifle and stout bullets, shooting this bull at the base of the tail will drop him in his tracks. However, the better option is to be patient and let him turn, giving you a quartering-away shot.

Spot & Stalk Secrets

It was cold just before dawn, the temperature a tad below freezing as the breeze tried to eat its way through my collar. I'd left the tent three hours earlier and was now nestled up against the trunk of an ancient spruce tree, impatiently waiting for it to get light enough to see through my binoculars.

As the day began to gray, I spotted some movement in the open park a quarter mile below. As it got lighter, the ghostlike shapes became elk bodies as the herd continued to feed. I grabbed my .300 Mag. and bumped down the slope to a spot 250 yards from the park, found a good rifle rest and got set up as I continued to glass. Soon I could see the antlers of several bulls among the 50-odd elk in the basin. One of those bulls was a nice 6x6 that soon wore my tag.

Out West, glassing for game—commonly called spot-and-stalk hunting—is the way most hunters pursue elk, deer, pronghorns and bears. The nature of this big country makes it much easier to cover ground quickly with your eyes instead of your legs. Then, when you locate game, you plan your stalk, move in and make the shot. In theory,

it's simple. In practice, there are several little tricks of the trade that will help you locate—and get shots at—more elk.

Prime Time

When I was first learning to hunt the West, an old sourdough once told me there are only two things you have to know to kill deer and elk consistently—sit on your behind and glass, and don't be afraid of the dark. After 30 years of hunting around the world, I can see how right he was.

I've met a lot of hunters who refused to hike to and from camp in the dark. Maybe they were afraid of the bogeyman. More likely, they did not have confidence in their skills and feared getting lost. As a result, they saw much less game and scored less often than those hunters who overcame their fears. (See "Let Them Do the Work," pages 106–108.)

The reason is simple: Deer, elk and other ungulates are what biologists call *crepuscular*, defined as "being active in the twilight." Their eyes are built so that they actually see better in twilight than they do at other times. That's one reason they're most active just before—and just after—it's barely light enough for us to see, and after dark. Also, once hunting pressure accelerates in a given area, elk are more likely to move and feed only at night. In these areas, "prime time" is the first 30 minutes you can see in the morning and the last 30 minutes you can see in the evening; these are the two times your chances of spotting elk moving in open areas are best.

I'll do whatever it takes to be in position to glass at prime time. Often this means hiking in the dark for an hour or more, using a flashlight or moonlight to get to and from my glassing station. I can't tell you how many times I've left camp at 3:00 a.m. to begin climbing to my glassing station. That sleeping bag sure is warm and nice, but if I had wanted warm and nice I would never have left home. I always think to myself—I'm here to shoot elk, and the best way to do that is to find them. The odds increase exponentially when you hunt during prime time.

Elk hunters need the best optics they can afford, with an emphasis on high-quality glass and binoculars that will gather the maximum amount of light at dawn and dusk, when elk are most active.

Where & How to Look

You need a good vantage point that permits you to look over maximum country when glassing. That generally means climbing to a high point overlooking a valley or finding a spot that allows you to glass into the timbered pockets on the opposite ridge. As it grays up in the morning, concentrate on open parks and meadows. These areas reflect a lot of available light, making it easy to see in them first. As it gets lighter, if you don't see any elk in these openings, start glassing the edges and into the timber—looking for trails, small meadows and saddles and the elk that frequent these places.

Get comfortable, sit down and rest your elbows on your knees as you glass. You need to keep your optics as steady as possible, to reduce eyestrain. Plus, standing will only cause rapid fatigue and not let you really "see" the country. Many people use a grid pattern, starting on one side of the area, sweeping their binoculars across it, raising them a bit, then sweeping back. If they don't see anything, they do it again. You have to have both faith in your spot and patience to continue glassing when no elk appear. Sometimes it pays to move 50 to 100 yards along your ridgetop to give you a different angle.

During midday, concentrate glassing efforts into the timber. Look for the shiny bodies of

How to Judge Bulls in the Field

He's not big, but he could be your only chance. Decide!

To the deer hunter who has never hunted elk before, even average bulls will look big. A 2½-year-old "brush bull"—an elk with a willowy four- or five-point rack of small size—will still carry more antler than the largest whitetail.

Let me also say that finding a bull that will meet the Boone and Crockett Club's minimum score of 375 points is as rare as finding a four-leaf clover. Only a handful are taken each season, with most coming from expensive private-land hunting areas. In most public land areas of the West, a 6x6 bull that scores 300 B&C points is considered a real dandy today, with a bull over 330 points truly the elk of a lifetime.

A trophy-class bull will have six or more long points per side (bulls with more than six points per side are extremely rare). Overall, the rack should be massive. The best bulls have antler bases that are hard to get one of your hands around, and this weight should be carried throughout. The first two points should appear to reach almost to the bull's nose. The third point should be nearly as long as the first two, and it's often here that good bulls lose much of their stature. The fourth point, also called the sword point, is the rack's most impressive. It should be long and thick and often measures more than 16 inches in length. Above the sword point the rack should fork, like the bifurcation of a mule deer's rack, with the remaining two points both longish and heavy.

This is a good bull in anybody's book.

In addition to point length and mass, the best bulls have an antler spread of at least 36 inches—preferably more. The main beam on true trophy bulls measures over 4 feet long, with a beam length of over 50 inches exceptional. When viewed broadside, the largest bulls have main beams that look like they can be used to scratch the elk's hindquarters.

When hunting elk, you need to be realistic. If you're hunting a general hunt on one of the West's public land areas, any branch-antlered bull is indeed a good one. In many special-draw units managed for trophy potential, a hunter may want to pass on young brush bulls in the hopes of finding something with larger antlers. Certainly, on private-land hunts where access is limited and hunting pressure tightly controlled, the chances for larger bulls increases and you may want to be picky. However, when discussing elk hunting with novices, I always try to stress the fact that the gods of the hunt are more fickle in elk hunting than in any other big-game hunting I've ever done. When you pass a shot at any legal bull today, do so knowing that your chances of filling your tag may have just walked off into the dark timber, never to reappear.

These bulls are huge, and your heart will nearly stop upon seeing one like this. Take your first good shot!

bedded elk along the edges of timber stringers. One time in Colorado, Dwight Schuh and I glassed up a dozen fat cow elk as they lazed in the sun on the edge of the timber a mile off, looking for all the world like beached whales as their bodies glistened in the light. By glassing across the valley into the timber on the other side, you can sometimes pick up elk as they move around in the trees. Glassing to determine where elk are bedding can be the first step in planning an ambush or drive.

During prime time I let my glasses jump around more, because I know elk should be moving, and by rapidly covering the country I up my chances of spotting movement. During midday, however, I slow the pace way down, picking apart the countryside as I look not for an elk but a piece of an elk, something that appears out of place. When I see something like this, I pull out the spotting scope and examine it closely.

The Value of Quality Optics

The importance of using only the very best optics you can afford cannot be overstated. Top-quality glass eliminates eyestrain, produces a clear, sharp image even "way out there" and pulls every last bit of light out of early dawn and dusk, when elk are most active. Names like Bausch & Lomb, Leica, Swarovski, Zeiss and Leupold will never disappoint you, even though they cost a fair chunk of change.

Binoculars in the 7X to 10X range are standard out West. Bring those that can use a lot of light, meaning glass with a large objective lens in relation to power. 7X35, 8X30, 8X40, 10X40 and 10X50 binoculars are large and somewhat heavy but worth every ounce. If you choose to pack a spotting scope, those with variable eyepieces in the 15-45X and 20-60X class are best.

Glassing should be part of every elk hunter's repertoire. Make sure you're on station at prime time, be meticulous in your search and bring along quality optics; you'll increase your odds for success tenfold.

No matter what, keep your optics steady to reduce eyestrain.

Look for Pieces & Parts

That is an important point to remember. Elk are big; it's true. But so is the country. You still have to look for "pieces and parts"—ear, head, cocked leg, horizontal backline, flicking tail, etc.—not a whole elk dallying in the open; you just won't see that very often.

THE DARK TIMBER

There are few times when an Eastern whitetail deer-hunting mentality—move agonizingly slowly, watch and listen before taking another step—is beneficial when elk hunting. Usually elk hunters are rewarded for covering ground and trying to locate pockets of elk.

But then there are those large stands of thick trees, impenetrable brush and log blow-downs known as the dark timber. The dark timber can be your ace in the hole, a place where pressured cows and bulls worn down from the rut go to get away from all those other hunters carelessly polluting the mountains with their sound and scent.

Dark timber is a bugger to hunt, but it can pay off.

WHEN TO HUNT THE DARK TIMBER

I try to avoid hunting the dark timber whenever possible. Why? Because it is very difficult to

move around in and twice as hard to hunt. It's thick, it's tough to stay quiet and, if you're not careful, the jumbles of fallen trees, slippery rocks and face-slapping brush will cause you to fall down, twist an ankle or worse. And heaven help you if you shoot an elk here. Getting it out is anything but pleasant.

Still, when I find plenty of elk sign but no elk, or when I can find cows but no bulls, I know it's time to suck it up and slip into the dark timber.

How to Hunt Dark Timber Pockets

Hunting dark timber is not rocket science, but more an exercise in stubbornness. The basic plan goes like this: Arrive on glassing station before first light, then glass and listen for elk during the first two hours. Nothing? Then use your scouting—which hopefully has shown you tracks, trails and wallows—as a guide to the dark timber canyons and hillsides where the most fresh sign is.

It takes patience, persistence and a keen sense of direction to successfully hunt the dark timber pockets bull elk love.

Leave all your unnecessary equipment in camp. I bring a small fleece daypack or fanny pack with water, lunch, flagging and meat care tools; and my weapon, map, compass, GPS and binoculars. Get the wind right and keep a wind-checker (butane lighter or puff bottle) in your pocket where you can reach and use it frequently. Find a tracked-up trail into the dark timber, and begin still-hunting.

Once inside the dark timber, look for pieces of an elk, not necessarily the whole elk body. You will often see the dark neck or light tan rump patch first, or antler tines, ears and—if you get down on your hands and knees, as you sometimes have to do to look under the thick brush—legs. Use your binoculars to give you a microscopic view of the woods as you try to pick out an elk.

As you move along, keep an eye out for terrain features that lend themselves to bedding areas. Elk use the dark timber primarily as bedding grounds, so look for benches and flats where the animals can rest comfortably. Remember that edge cover is an elk attractant here just as it is on the outside, only on a smaller scale. A small meadow bordered by thick brush, a jumble of fallen trees adjacent to standing timber or a creek channel or shallow ravine bordered by a brushy flat are all good places for elk to bed.

Be Safe & Stay Alert

While your goal is to spot the elk while they're still bedded, often you'll end up jumping them. My friend Rick Wemple, a superb elk guide from Victor, Montana, and I still-hunted some dark timber hellholes in Idaho's Selway Wilderness Area one hot October week. We did spot a few elk in their beds, but usually after a couple of hours of nothing, we'd jump a lone bull up out of his bed at very close range. They were small bulls, so we never shot, but we always got on them long enough to make that shot had we chosen to do so.

These elk would jump up and bound off, but they invariably hesitated after a few yards, long enough for me to put the crosshairs on them. When still-hunting the dark timber, you need to do so with the rifle at port arms *at all times*, ready to shoot. Also, make sure you've stopped and glassed ahead thoroughly before taking each step.

You don't have to move quite as slowly here as you do hunting deer. As is the case with all elk hunting, the more ground you can cover, the better off you'll be. After a time you'll begin recognizing places that just look and feel "elky." *That* is the time to slow the pace way down and use your fine-tooth comb.

The dark timber is full of "gotchas." Be careful and safe when hunting here. Taking a compass reading from time to time, especially when on flat ground, will help prevent you from getting

When hunting the dark timber, move slowly while carefully looking ahead for a piece of a bedded bull. Often you'll only see antler tips, the flick of an ear or a horizontal backline in a sea of vertical brush.

turned around and lost. (It can happen!) Also—take a GPS reading from a recognizable vantage point, before heading in. Because you'll have to keep a round in the chamber and the rifle on safety, you have to be extra careful not to fall. Make sure your scope is turned down to its lowest power setting, too, as you'll never get a shot over 50 to 75 yards in the dark timber. More likely, a shot will be 50 to 75 *feet*. When you shoot an elk, be sure you flag the spot and your trail back out of the brush, or use your GPS. And, while you're hunting, always be alert for potential ambush spots—wallows, tracked-up trail intersections and the like—places where you might come back and build a ground blind or set a treestand.

Hunting the dark timber isn't for everyone. But every now and then you have to go in and root the elk out. When the going gets tough, the tough (and stubborn!) head for the dark timber. Often, that's where success lies, in the form of a big, bedded bull elk.

Pressure-Cooked Elk

These days, it's getting tough to find a "secret spot" to hunt elk. Even many backcountry areas well away from roads are hunted by outfitters, private individuals with horses or pack llamas, and enterprising backpackers. The proliferation of ATVs and four-wheel-drive vehicles means that virtually every logging road open for motorized travel during hunting season has more than its share of hunters.

Taken together, that means there are a whole lot of elk out there that have become hunter-wise in a big way. They react to this influx of humanity in a predictable way: They run scared. It quickly becomes difficult to find them. But don't despair. You can still harvest an elk when the pressure's on. To do so you'll have to modify standard hunting tactics, try a few new tricks and—how do I say this tactfully?—get a bit lucky. Here's a plan.

Finding Elk

When I plan an elk hunt, one of the things I try to anticipate is hunter pressure. Will there be lots of other hunters? Where will they likely be coming from? How will they be hunting? When the people move in, what will the elk do? Where will elk go, and how will they get there?

Like pressured deer, elk often do one of two things when the pressure increases. They become increasingly nocturnal in their movements—doing the bulk of their feeding, watering and traveling either on the cusp of daylight or after dark. Or they head for the safest places they can find within their range. These are usually the dark timber hellholes found at the bottoms of roadless vertical canyons and ravines, jungles of brush on steep hillsides and the like.

To find them, you have to do what they do. That means glassing as early and as late as possible and being willing to hunt the nasty stuff. (See "Spot & Stalk Hunting" and "The Dark Timber.") You also have to be willing to try to find pockets of solitude where other hunters may not have been yet, or haven't discovered.

"Unpressured" Pressured Elk

Pockets of solitude, where elk may have moved to after being chased around by other hunters, are excellent places to fill a tag. Sometimes it takes a little imagination to figure them out. Here are two examples.

In southwestern Montana, there is an area where elk migrate out of Yellowstone National Park onto national forest lands starting in August with the rut. Hunters understand this and often line up near the park boundary line, anticipating new elk coming onto land open to hunting. But the majority of the elk travel after dark, slipping through this gauntlet unseen. They move several miles along the spine of the mountain, away from the park border and onto roadless areas where hunting access is tough for even the fittest hunter. Once the elk reach this area, they calm down and begin acting like normal elk again. Hunters who have figured out this pattern are able to slip into the country and hunt these elk without interference from others who continue waiting for those few elk that leave the park during legal shooting hours.

In many Western states there are large areas of high-elevation public lands fronted for miles by private ranches that refuse to allow the public access through their property to the national forest lands. These public land tracts often hold good numbers of elk, especially after the shooting starts on nearby areas that are easily accessible by hunters.

How can you gain access to these public land hot spots?

Two ways. The simplest, and most painful, is to walk into the national forest on obvious public trailheads, then pack the several miles into the mountains behind these ranches. The second involves researching public easements, which are access corridors sometimes found through private lands but only lightly publicized, if at all. The local U.S.D.A. Forest Service or Bureau of Land Management (BLM) office may be able to point these out to you, but the surest place is the local county courthouse, where meticulous records of private property ownership and public land access are kept. Plat maps will show you exact borders, which you can transfer onto your own topographic maps. These are invaluable for access purposes and so you won't inadvertently trespass on private land. You need to know this because you'll probably be hunting close to the property boundary. The elk, more than likely, will be feeding at least part of the time in the rancher's fields, then moving onto public timber lands to bed.

When there are lots of hunters afield, it gets tougher and tougher to fill your tag. Every year, though, a handful of enterprising hunters beat those odds and put elk meat in the freezer. Sometimes they just get lucky, but more often than not they make their own luck by hunting harder, hunting smarter and looking for those precious little pockets of solitude where elk go to escape the horde of blaze orange.

There's no reason you can't do the same thing too.

When hunting pressure is high, smart hunters use their topographic maps to try to find escape routes, isolated hellholes and areas where most other hunters can't, or won't, go. You can be sure those are the places the elk have gone.

Let Them Do the Work

In areas of high hunter pressure, you can often turn the crowds into allies, not adversaries, by setting up so they will drive the elk right past your stand. The key? Get up there early—way before the crowds—and watch closely because the elk will slip through quietly.

One year in Colorado, I thought I had it figured out. I drove out to my hunting area two days before the rifle season opened, and there wasn't another soul in sight. I joyously set up camp, then scouted both days, locating two herds of elk. Man, I thought, this is great!

The night before the opener the other hunters started arriving in droves. Where did they all come from? The dirt road leading to camp looked like an L.A. freeway during rush hour. Rats, I remember thinking. Now what?

Outsmart the Hunters, Outsmart the Elk

Instead of giving up, I did what I always do when it gets like that—I decided to let the other hunters work for me, not against me.

On opening morning, I grudgingly crawled out of my sleeping bag at 2:00 a.m., ate a cold breakfast, grabbed my rifle and pack and quietly started up the mountain by flashlight. I kept a low profile, careful not to let the other camps see or hear me. It took three hours of hard climbing, but by 5:30 a.m. I was set up in a saddle 2,500 feet above the valley floor. My perch overlooked two long, deep timbered canyons, both of which had well-used elk trails coming out of the top of the timber stringers that led into my saddle. I had stumbled across this spot during my scouting, and it was obvious that here was a natural pathway for the elk to travel between one drainage and the next.

How to Intercept Pressured Elk

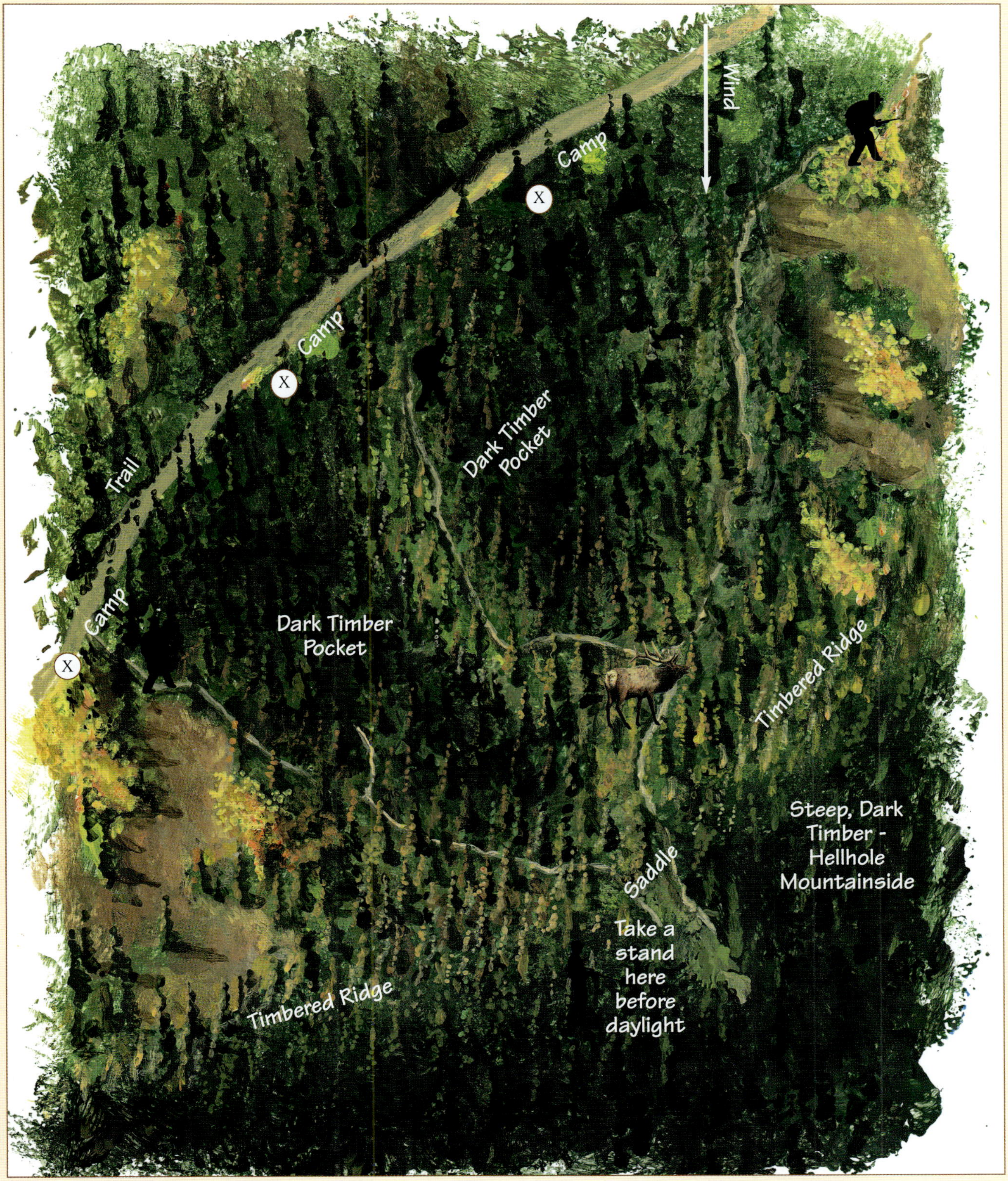

When the woods are alive with other hunters during the general firearms season, it is often best to let the hordes of other hunters work for you, not against you. Sometimes you have to leave camp hours before daylight, climbing in the dark by flashlight to reach a saddle through which escaping elk may travel as they elude the onslaught of advancing hunters and head for the safety of the dark timbered hellhole on the other side. Remember: It's better to be 30 minutes early than 5 minutes late. Set up on the downwind side of the saddle where you can watch open pockets in the timber and the trails leading to, and passing through, the saddle.

I found an old log to lie behind, over which I first set my daypack, then rested my rifle. I took a long drink of water, dug my binoculars out and got ready. An hour or so before daylight, the sounds of walking hunters traveled up the slope (it always amazes me how far sound travels in the mountains). As soon as it got gray enough to see, I spotted my first elk in small open pockets about halfway down the slope. Far below, I could soon see several orange vests working their way up the slope. I was reminded of the massed charges infantrymen made on entrenched positions during the Civil War and, like the hunters below, how futile their efforts usually were.

During the first 30 minutes of light I saw no fewer than 75 elk—mostly cows, calves and small bulls—as they worked their way up and across the slope, most passing through my saddle into the safety of the next drainage. Then, out of nowhere, a very nice, heavy-antlered 5x5 bull led a small procession of six elk into the saddle at a trot. The 75-yard shot was a gimme.

Rocket Science? I Don't Think So!

This isn't rocket science. That morning I had two choices—beat my head against a big rock and hunt with the masses (with minuscule odds for success), or let the other hunters work for me, not against me ... in essence becoming a large herd of beaters driving the elk right past my hiding spot.

The key is to recognize the opportunity when it arises and, through scouting or knowledge of the terrain, determine where the elk are likely to move once they're spooked and begin to escape to greener pastures. The same scenario has played itself over for me many other times in similar, though not exactly the same, fashion. Whenever possible, it's advantageous to set up above the elk and the other hunters and to play the wind. It's always helpful if nobody sees you take your stand. Under these circumstances, even when not required by law, I always wear lots of blaze orange, for obvious reasons.

Who says you have to join the crowd? I'd rather beat 'em instead by letting them do the hard work. After all, the meat packing work was all downhill!

When the Snow Flies

Make no mistake about it—the epitome of elk hunting is the early fall, when the aspen leaves are turning yellow and frosty mountain meadows ring with the sound of the elk's bugle. This is a magical time, and no one who longs to hunt elk should miss it.

However, the bugling period and the often-dead time immediately following the rut are not necessarily the best times of year to take a monster bull. In fact, they may not be the best times of year to take any elk, be it bull or cow. "Prime time" to harvest an elk is very late in the year, after the snows of winter have begun to fall, temperatures have dropped below freezing—sometimes below 0°F—and the elk have begun moving down out of the high country into their winter range.

It is snow—I mean serious, deep snow that stays until the following spring and can reach

Hunting Migrating Elk

Hunting the late-season winter migration from summer to winter range can be the absolute best time to find a large bull. When the snows get deep enough, the elk will leave the high country near timberline and filter down through the timbered mountainsides toward winter range. This winter range can be on both public land and private ranch lands, especially those with alfalfa fields. To find elk when they're moving, you can glass from the lowland area, often from your vehicle off public roads. Look for elk and fresh tracks in the snow as the elk begin traveling from timberline and above (A) down obvious game trails (B) and feeding in open grassy meadows and parks (C) located on the timbered mountainsides. Spot the elk late in the evening, marking their location and knowing they'll be down on the edge of an open park. Then climb to that park in the dark the next morning, getting into position to ambush the elk as they feed into the park at first light before moving on.

above an elk's belly line—that spurs the annual exodus of elk herds from the high mountains. In this the elk have no choice. They must leave to be able to find enough high-quality food to sustain them until the warmth of spring (a *long* time away) brings forth fresh new grasses.

This annual migration has a profound impact on elk herds. In some high country areas, elk basically have two different home range territories—summer range and winter range. Summer range is always much larger and encompasses the high mountain meadows and steep timbered mountainsides. But when the snows come, elk are forced to lower elevations—flatter ground where they can paw through the snow to find food. Generally speaking, winter range makes up 10 percent or less of an elk herd's yearly habitat. This smaller total habitat area obviously will concentrate the elk, making them easier for you to locate.

Of course, in southern areas like Arizona and much of New Mexico, elk do not need to migrate from summer to winter range. In these states, there are fewer advantages of hunting in the late season because the elk can stay high virtually all year around. But when hunting the northern elk ranges, it is wise to consider trying to hunt during the winter migration, if at all possible.

Migration Hunts

Practically overnight, bulls, cows and calves begin appearing near roads and trailheads and in ranchers' hay fields when the migration begins. No longer does the hunter have to be half mountain man to reach the secluded high-altitude rough country elk prefer during the general seasons. It becomes much easier to find them and, once found and harvested, to get the meat back to civilization.

That's not to say it's always a cakewalk. Usually you'll end up slogging through snow—often very deep snow—and fighting bitter temperatures and icy winds. But when the elk get closer to the roads, the hunting is always easier.

One problem in hunting the migration is that it can never be timed exactly, like the solstice or the return of the swallows to Capistrano. However, elk generally follow the same historic routes year in and year out, and some elk will come down out of the high country about the same time each year. Without the deep snow, though, most elk—and almost all the bigger bulls—stay high until forced to come lower.

The amount of snow needed to move elk depends on the distance they need to travel to reach their wintering grounds. If they have no more than a few miles to go, they are more likely to stay high longer. Elk that have to travel 40 or 50 miles—as many herds do—will depart the high country more quickly. As they move, the elk will cover many miles each day, often stopping for a few days in small pockets of habitat that have good forage. Again, the amount of snow is the driving force.

How to Hunt Deep Snow

There are two basic ways to hunt the deep snow. The first is the standard spot-and-stalk technique. Climb high to a good vantage point before daylight, put on your warm clothes and use your binoculars to spot elk as they travel or feed at first light. They often stay out later in the morning now than they do earlier in the fall, simply because they have to eat more to stay warm. This is a decided advantage for glassers.

As for the second way to hunt deep snow: If I don't find what I want by glassing, I do what I really like to do this time of year—pick up a fresh track in the snow and follow it.

This sounds simple, but it usually ends in failure. Unless the snow is powdery quiet, the elk will hear you coming. The wind, which can help cover up your noisy crunching, must be steady to prevent elk from smelling you. But since the elk is walking and you have to follow his tracks, you can't be too choosy about wind direction. Try climbing above the track, keeping it in sight as you follow, which will help you see down into the trees and brush and hopefully spot the animal more quickly. Always move slowly in the timber, using your binoculars to glass for pieces of standing or bedded elk. Of course, even if the track is very fresh, the elk may be miles ahead of you, and you'll never catch him.

When hunting the winter migration, climbing high to a good vantage point and glassing for herds of traveling elk is an excellent method. Dress warmly and be prepared to stay on the mountain all day.

Cow calling can be helpful when tracking elk in snow, especially if you bump them but they haven't smelled or seen you. Often, soft cow calling will draw the herd back to you, giving you a chance to pick out a fat cow or bull to wear your tag.

Where to Hunt?

The biggest problem in hunting the migration is finding a place to hunt. At present, with the exception of Montana—in which the general rifle elk season runs through the end of November—other elk states close their seasons before the snows have usually come in strong enough to move the elk. Many states do offer special-draw tags for the late season, but they are extremely difficult to draw. Start applying, earning preference points if possible, and keep on applying.

Prime areas to hunt during the migration are adjacent to national parks, where special late-season tags allow hunting for elk that are protected inside park boundaries but whose winter range is outside the park. Wyoming's Yellowstone National Park and Alberta's Banff National Park are prime examples. Finding exact migration corridors is as easy as asking a local game warden or game department biologist. These routes are no deep, dark secret, and the officials' objective *is* harvesting excess elk.

Also, I've spotted many late-season elk from a truck parked on a highway or paved county road, using a spotting scope and window mount to glass long distances into the mountains at first and last light for both elk and elk tracks. I like to spot in the evenings. That way, if I see bulls I want to hunt, I find they'll usually be close to that same spot in the morning. So, I bite the bullet and leave camp many hours before sunup and begin trudging up the mountain in the deep snow, hoping to reach the area where I last saw those elk before first light. If things work out—and they have, many times—I spot the bulls as they feed in the same general area first thing in the morning.

Many a big bull is taken by hardy hunters willing to overcome the difficulties of hunting thigh-deep snow in bitter cold. In winter, when things are right, you will have the best chance you'll ever have of taking a monster bull. If that thought doesn't keep you warm, perhaps you should take up knitting.

The very best time of the year to harvest an elk of any kind, including a trophy-class bull, is after the snow flies. Deep snows get the elk moving out of their high-elevation strongholds and down into more accessible lowland areas. This photo doesn't condone road hunting, but it does demonstrate how far down elk will come to escape a high-country winter.

Chapter 7

RADICAL ELK STRATEGIES

It never fails. You thought you had a foolproof plan, but it didn't work. Why did the elk fail to cooperate? The weather? Other hunters? Just because they didn't? Whatever the reason, it's back to square one.

While there have been millions of words written by a lot of very good elk hunters telling you how to be successful at this often-maddening game, the fact of the matter is that elk rarely play by the rules. If they are anything, an elk is fickle: a here-today-gone-tomorrow tan ghost that can make a monkey out of the toughest and most highly skilled woodsman. Those elk hunting videos where the big bulls come charging in like clockwork and get themselves shot at close range in broad daylight? Sure, it happens. For someone else. But when it comes to you and me, fuhgedaboudit!

So when the going gets tough, it's time to improvise ... to reach deep down into your bag of tricks and go for greatness. It's time to roll the dice, take a chance, hit a 16, try to fill an inside straight. Take your experiences as a successful turkey hunter and apply them to calling elk. Get aggressive and go for the gold.

If I've learned one thing over three decades of elk hunting, it's this: When it's not happening, make it happen! Go get 'em. Don't sit back and wonder what happened. Attack! Because when you become aggressive, yet attack under control, you'll start to regain control of the situation. You'll know that—win or lose—you've given it your best shot. And even in defeat you'll learn valuable lessons about elk that simply cannot be learned any other way.

And remember, always have fun. It may be frustrating, and it's certainly always hard work, but if it's not fun, why be there? And what better way to have fun than to beat an elk on your own terms, on the elk's ground, doing it your way ...

Turkey-Hunting Strategies—For Elk

Many first-time elk hunters are from east of the Mississippi River, where they have some experience hunting wild turkeys. One way for these hunters to minimize the learning curve on their initial attempt at elk hunting is to use their turkey-hunting skills as a basis for pursuing elk. David Hale, half of the famous Knight & Hale game-calling team and a master at both disciplines, explains how to make the transition:

"Elk hunting is an advanced course in turkey-hunting tactics and techniques. The steep mountains and larger home area of elk make it physically more challenging. But you can apply basic turkey-hunting skills to elk hunting and become successful early on."

"The key," Hale says, "is to respect the strong points of the elk (its sense of smell and good eyesight) and attack its weak points (its hearing and, at the right time of year, the breeding urge)."

Hunting the Rut

During the pre-rut, Hale recommends bugling to locate bulls, then cow calling to attack them. "The earliest bugling is just the bulls sounding off, feeling their oats," he says. "The big boys probably won't come to you, but you can use the bugle to get them to sound off and reveal their whereabouts, then sneak in closer. Once in close, cow calls can bring them in." Hale likens these bugles, which he calls "shock bugles," to the shock gobble used in turkey hunting.

During the peak of the rut, bulls have their cows already rounded up and are reluctant to leave them to take on a challenging, bugling bull—or hunter. This is the time to use mating calls, including both the cow call and what has been termed the "excited" cow call (see chapter 4), which imitates a cow elk at the peak of her estrus cycle. "Excited cow calling involves making a series of excited mews, chirps and squeals," Hale explains, "just like the excited yelps, cuts and the fighting purr work at the same time on turkeys.

"The secret," Hale reveals, "is to get a bull so worked up that he will make a mistake, which is coming over to the excited cow sounds you're making, and try to round you up to be part of his harem. This works on both the more dominant herd bulls, as well as the younger satellite bulls that are always circling a herd of cows during the rut." Hale compares the antics of satellite bull elk to jake turkeys.

During the post-rut period, Hale recommends using a call as a primary tool for locating bulls, then moving in as silently as possible. "After the rut, the bulls are worn out and tired," he explains. "They've been chased by hunters blowing calls out of control, too. They aren't going to come to your calls, but they may answer once or twice, which is all you need to pinpoint their location and plan a stalk."

Once you get a bull to answer you during post-rut conditions, Hale recommends getting quickly into position. "Often the elk will be moving away from you, wanting to be left alone," he describes. "You have to anticipate their line of travel and, often, run as fast as you can to get ahead of them." The same can be said of an old gobbler that won't come to your calls but instead travels on a line away from your position. Once you're close, a single soft cow call or yelp can often bring the bull or gobbler those few steps closer needed to get an open shot.

"Hunting rutting elk is an advanced course in spring turkey hunting," says call maker David Hale, a veteran elk and turkey hunter. "The key is to stay flexible, using your turkey hunting experiences as your guide even if you've never hunted elk before."

Stay Flexible

Hale emphasizes the need to remain flexible in your approach to hunting both elk and turkeys. "It is very important to be able to adjust your plan according to the movements of the elk or turkeys and to make your own moves based on what is happening at any given moment," he advises. "Too many hunters do the same thing day in and day out, falling into a pattern of doing something that may have worked for them once, but isn't

"Gobbling" for Elk

Elk Sounds	Turkey Sounds	Hunting Purpose	How to Approach Them
Cow call	Yelp	Pre-mating contact sounds are useful for locating animals.	Slip in as close as possible while remaining undetected.
"Shock" Bugle	"Shock" Gobble	This pre-rut call is used to locate animals that will answer but won't always come to your aggressive calling.	Once located, switch to "sexy" sounds of cow or hen.
Mating Sounds ("Hyper-Hot" cow call)	Mating Sounds (excited hen calls, cutting sounds)	Breeding season is here. Gobblers have hens; bulls have cows. Neither want to leave their females to come to you.	Gobblers and bulls will both hang up. The excited calls can bring the entire flock or herd to you; if so, males will follow. Calls will also readily draw in jakes and satellite bulls. Try to get males excited enough to make a mistake.
Soft Calls (cow calls, chirps, mews)	Soft Calls (clucks, purrs)	Use when a gobbler or bull comes towards you, but hangs up 50–100 yards off. Use calls sparingly.	The rut is winding down and males are tired. Soft calls may get them to come the extra few yards needed to offer a shot. Watch for animals that come in silently.
Shock Bugle	Shock Gobble	Use during post-rut blues time. Animals are unlikely to come to aggressive mating calls and may even leave when you call to them.	Try to shock the animal into calling once, revealing its location; then move quickly to try to get close to it and in front of its line of travel. Then, one soft cluck or mew might move it close enough for a shot, or into the open.

necessarily what is going to work for them today. To be consistently successful, you have to be able to adapt your techniques and tactics—often several times during a single encounter."

Honor the Senses

"With elk, you have to watch the wind every second or you're history," Hale emphasizes. "Because elk are noisy animals, you can run—even breaking branches and stomping your feet—to get the wind right and get away with it ... if they don't see you move. But if they see you, it's all over. You have to be especially careful that a cow or satellite bull doesn't bust you, too." With turkeys, the wind is not a factor, but staying hidden is. "With turkeys, the ambush you set has to be more passive, with less movement," Hale says. "With elk, the ambush can be more active as you move to get into position."

Use Your Experiences

"Novice elk hunters can use their turkey hunting experiences as a basis for elk hunting. This is a great way to get started in an unfamiliar type of hunting," Hale recommends. "Just remember that elk are the same, only different. You always have to be ready to adjust in the middle of the hunt and be willing to learn new tricks every time you're in the woods. That's the best way to become a consistently successful elk hunter."

This elk is ready to bust you. Be ultra-careful: Practice calling before the hunt, use the wind, wear full camouflage, keep movement to a minimum, get ready to shoot only when he's not looking ... just like turkey hunting!

Throw Out the Textbook

The more you hunt elk, the more you realize that there is no one magic formula for success. In fact, elk hunting can be one of the most frustrating of all North American big-game hunting challenges simply because no two elk hunts are ever the same. On most elk hunts, I've discovered that no two days are ever the same, either.

This means that to be consistently successful, elk hunters must be willing to adapt their techniques and hunting styles to the conditions at hand. Hunters must be able to shift gears in mid-hunt, forsaking their favorite technique and doing whatever it takes to get a shot.

That's where radical elk strategies come into play. My attitude is simple. If the elk won't play by the rule book, why should I?

Controlled Aggression

Many novice elk hunters are deer hunters out trying to find an elk. They forget that elk are not deer and that passive techniques that can be deadly on the smartest whitetail buck will impress bull elk not one whit.

My own style of throw-out-the-textbook elk hunting is one I call "controlled aggression." It has been so successful for me that I have adapted it to virtually all my big-game hunting, regardless of the species being pursued or the weapon I'm using. After losing opportunities at several good bulls over the years by waiting for something to happen that never did, my attitude now is to make it happen. I'd rather blow a shot opportunity by being a bit too aggressive than lose that same opportunity by being too passive. Being bold—but not too bold—has been the key to lots of elk hunting success for me.

When elk hunting, I travel as quickly as possible through the woods looking for elk or hot elk sign. Heck, sometimes I even dogtrot. Honest! I want to cover maximum territory in minimum time. When I spot elk or stumble across fresh sign, I slow down and start actually "hunting." And it seems that whenever I find the elk, things are never textbook perfect. That's when I have to make something happen. Earlier, in "When They Won't Come," I described using a fake elk antler as a sort of decoy to lure in a hung-up bull during a calling confrontation. That's a good example of controlled aggression. Another is "The Flush."

The Buddy System, employing a stationary caller and an attacking archer, is one of the deadliest methods ever devised for taking bull elk during the rut. This archer is getting ready to move out toward the bull ... if he hangs up and doesn't come in to the calling.

The Flush

One time my buddy and I were stalking a herd of elk through heavy timber during the tail end of the rut. These elk wouldn't come to our calling, and the nature of the terrain and shifting winds made crawling in close to them impossible. So we decided to take a page from fall turkey hunting and flush them. We spread 50 yards apart and sprinted downhill, right into the herd, bugling like a pair of satellite bulls with overactive testes. The cows, of course, scattered like hen turkeys, taking the two good bulls with them as they thundered off down the slope. It was the Charge of the Light Brigade!

My buddy and I followed them for a quarter mile as quietly as we could, then set up and began a series of cow and calf calling, alternating with silence. It took 45 minutes, but suddenly a single cow appeared. Then another, and another, and another. Soon there were cows everywhere, and soon the bulls came, trusting in the judgment of those cows. Eddie arrowed a dandy six-point that day.

"The Flush" doesn't always work. In fact, it's a good way to run the elk into the next county. But sometimes it does work. It's a roll of the dice, the purchase of a lottery ticket. But when all else fails, if you're not going to get close anyway, why not try to make something happen?

Passive-Aggressive

Sometimes aggressively using a passive technique can pay off. Treestands are an example of this. We've already talked about using treestands passively over waterholes and wallows during the rut or during hot early-season weather. I have friends in Montana who glass elk from their trucks during late-season snows and, when the migration is on, simply set up treestands in funnel areas right in the migration route. They aggressively use their treestands, often packing them on their backs a mile or more up steep, snow-covered slopes. When they hit it right and the elk are moving, they often see a dozen or more bulls each day.

Another bunch of serious elk hunters I know like to listen for lots of bugling, then move into the area (which obviously holds several bulls) and aggressively scout it on the go. Then, before daylight, they'll seed a fresh wallow or bench full of fresh rubs with elk-in-heat scent, set a treestand and, at first light, use a combination of cow-in-heat calling and satellite bull squealing right from their elevated stands. If they can pack one to the area, they'll set an elk decoy. They're passively hunting from the trees, but they have aggressively tried to lure the elk within shooting distance.

You get the picture. When aggressively hunting in a controlled manner, the only limitations are your imagination, your ability to read the situation and your willingness to go with your gut feelings and break the rules. I've yet to meet an elk who has read the rule book. They'll never know you fudged—and I certainly won't tell.

The Buddy System

One of the most effective ways to work bull elk is in tandem, with one hunter the caller or decoy and the other the designated shooter. It's a fairly aggressive strategy, and here's how it works.

When a bull responds to your calling, he'll often come close but hang up 70 to 100 yards out. He wants to see another elk before committing to his path. One solution to this dilemma is to have one hunter set up and call, rake trees and continue working the bull, while the shooter slips ahead 50 to 100 yards, depending on the circumstances. The shooter must keep his or her eyes and ears open to avoid bumping the bull, and once it's obvious the elk is coming, determine its line of march and get set up in a hurry. If the caller knows where his partner is set up, the caller should try to create a straight line from his position through his buddy (the shooter) to the bull. That will usually draw the elk right to the shooter. Intent on the location of the caller, the bull, if the wind is right, will sometimes walk right past the shooter without a second glance, offering a good shot.

The buddy system also works well on herd bulls that continue bugling but won't leave their cows to come close enough to shoot. The caller simply stays put and calls, keeping the bull talking so the shooter will know exactly where he is while slipping in like a stealth bomber and trying to stalk in close enough for a shot.

There are many variations on the buddy-system theme, but one thing's for certain: When it comes to fooling bull elk, two heads are generally better than one—especially if they work together as a team.

One of the best ways to call elk in is using the buddy system. Here two hunters hear a bull bugle (A) and silently move down the slope to attack him (B). When they get near the creek (C), the caller remains near the water, calling and raking a tree to keep the bull excited and, as the bull continues to bugle, let the shooter know exactly where he is. The shooter (D) moves toward the bull, either trying to find him or, if the calling gets heated enough, set up and let the bull walk past him for a shot. If everything goes right, the bull's attention will be focused on the caller, and he'll have no idea there's a second hunter—until it's too late.

Chapter 8

Planning Your Hunt

It's true. Elk hunting can be physically and mentally demanding like no other big-game hunting challenge you'll ever face. And yet the toughest part of elk hunting is simply finding an elk. Period. To do that, you need to become a researcher.

It's what I term "shrink your focus." In a nutshell, that means you have to shrink your hunting plans, from first choosing a state to hunt elk in, down to a single mountain range in that state, then down to a specific drainage in that mountain range. You make your final choice based on information gleaned through your research. The same is true when choosing an outfitter for a guided hunt. You have to find someone who hunts in good elk country, has a solid track record and a long list of satisfied clients and, just as important, is the kind of person you're willing to risk your irreplaceable elk hunting trip with.

There are lots of places to glean information. In this chapter you'll find ways to find a good place to hunt on your own and recommendations on how to go about selecting an outfitter. There are telephone and fax numbers and Web site addresses for government offices that can help you, too, as well as places to find the maps you'll need.

You may be planning to hunt elk for a week, but in reality, if you want to be successful and you don't live in good elk country, your hunt will take much longer than that. It will begin in the dead of winter and encompass bits and pieces of your time from then until you finally arrive on site and set up your tent.

If you've done your homework, you'll be serenaded by the sound of bugling bulls or charmed by the sight of dozens of elk that first wonderful morning. If your luck holds, you'll be one of the fortunate hunters who get to tie their tag around the antlers of a good bull. Because you know, as the best elk hunters do, that you have to make your own luck in this game.

But you only get lucky by planning and researching. Here's how to go about it ...

The Importance of Research

The key to any serious on-your-own elk hunter's success, season after season, can be boiled down to two things—planning and hard work. Most hunters get so excited about the actual hunt itself that they forget that without proper planning and meticulous research, their hunt is doomed from the get-go. Once in the mountains, any success they may have will be the result of nothing more than blind luck. Are you willing to leave it to the tarot cards?

I'm not. That's why I am a researcher.

Elk hunting is a variation of the needle-in-a-haystack game. Elk hunters often forget that before they can shoot an elk, they first have to find one. And finding elk is by far the hardest part of the entire equation. Only very small pockets of mountain habitat hold elk herds at any given time, despite the fact that the entire

drainage might be good elk habitat. With limited hunting time, we all need to maximize the time we spend afield where the elk are, not where they might be. Research gets you started in the right direction. I look at it as a true part of the hunt—my first steps to my next elk!

Step One: Files

I have several different files at home that help me plan my hunts. Into my "elk" file each year goes all sorts of things—magazine articles, maps, harvest statistics, state game statistics, notes from books and more. I also have separate files for each elk state, into which goes the current year's hunting regulations and license and tag application procedures. These items help me decide on new areas I may want to hunt based on information on what's hot and what's not.

Keeping everything in organized file folders makes it easier for me to keep track of the several different hunting trips I'm planning for the coming year as well as hunts I'm dreaming about for future years.

Step Two: Game Departments

Contact the game departments of the states you're considering and get the coming year's regulations. Elk seasons vary widely by state, as do application procedures, due dates and costs. Ask the department if they have harvest statistics and tag-drawing odds summaries available. Many states do, for a slight fee. Spend the money and get one for each state. These numbers will help paint a broad portrait of hunter success and distribution, harvest by area, tag-drawing odds and trophy quality.

Step Three: Maps, Maps and More Maps

Once you've narrowed your choice of elk hunting areas down to a general location, it's time for maps. The U.S. Forest Service and Bureau of Land Management each have public land maps within specific states that help you locate boundaries, roads, water sources, timbered ridges, trails

Smart elk hunters begin researching their hunt right at home, using state game regulations, maps and other information sources to begin a telephone search for a productive hunting area.

and trail heads, campgrounds and more. I like general state maps, too, which show major roads and towns. Taken together, all these maps give me a good overview of the area I want to hunt.

Later in the process it will be time for U.S. Geological Survey topographic maps. These maps show too small an area for initial planning but are essential for the final planning and hunt execution phases of your trip. Hold off on buying them until you know where you'll be hunting. I use the larger maps to help me define the general area I want to hunt, then topo maps to show me exactly where I think the elk will be in the area, as well as how I will both access and attack the area.

I can't emphasize the importance of maps enough, both in planning and in the actual hunt itself. Without them I feel as blind as the proverbial bat.

Step Four: People

The final stage of the planning process is talking with people. Maps can give you a general overview of the area, but people can fill in the blanks and give you an accurate, up-to-the-minute picture of what the area is really like.

"Up-to-date" is the key phrase here. While maps are invaluable, you'll rarely find one that's up-to-date. New roads, towns, subdivisions, trails, logging operations, fires and so on may not be shown on maps, but local people may know about them and help you fill in the blanks.

Talk with state game department biologists whenever possible. When I talk to these folks, I

Finding a new place to hunt elk successfully is a game of gathering information. Studying regulation booklets and asking questions of knowledgeable local hunting shop personnel are two good places to begin the search.

try to work my way down—not up—the departmental flow chart. I don't want the person in charge of half the state—I want the local biologist for a specific forest or drainage I'm considering hunting. The same holds true for game wardens, forest service personnel and so on. These people work right in the area and can fill me in on current conditions and elk population numbers. They may be hard to locate and it might take several phone calls before you actually hook up with them once you've learned who they are, but it is time and money well spent.

Whenever possible, I also try to talk with local hunters, taxidermists and any other contacts I can think of. I try to ask as many people as I can the same question, then "balance" their answers in my mind.

Step Five: Topo Maps

About the time I start calling people, I like to buy topographic maps of the drainages that I'm pretty sure I'm going to hunt. Topo maps help me pinpoint specific creeks, drainages and ridges where my research tells me the elk should be when I arrive. Topo maps also allow me to ask the people I'm calling very specific questions about the area. I coat my topos with a clear waterproof sealer that I can write on, and I write notes on them during my research, detailing information I pick up talking with people. Topo maps help me narrow things down from general information on the elk herd to details like specific terrain features; areas that may receive lots of pressure from other hunters; areas nobody goes to because they're too rough and remote; or the best ways to access the hunting grounds. When I'm done with my research, my topo maps closely resemble those used in military operations.

Meticulous research. I know it isn't glamorous, and it sure isn't as exciting as having a big 6x6 bull, red eyes bugged out, slobbering all over you at 10 yards in a rut-crazed frenzy. But truth be known, I enjoy it. It's all part of the chess game, a way to tip the odds for success in your favor and to keep the fire burning during the off-season. You get to talk hunting with other folks, maybe even make some new friends.

Maps are the key both to maneuvering around the backcountry and in planning and executing a wilderness elk hunt. You should never head afield without topographic maps of your hunting area.

No, research is not foolproof. That's why it's a part of hunting. Research is hard work, but you can make it fun, and it sure beats stumbling around the mountains like some clueless city boy waiting for the prize patrol to arrive with the envelope.

How to Draw the Best in the West

Competition for game is becoming more intense every year on our public lands. As more and more ranchers are either posting "No Hunting" signs or leasing their hunting rights to outfitters or small groups of well-heeled businessmen, private lands are becoming more difficult for the unattached hunter to access. As a result, the unattached hunter is often squeezed in during seasons that are often too short, with truckloads of others in the same boat. The result

is that trophy quality in many areas is going down along with success rates. And the chances of experiencing what many of us deem a quality hunting experience—good numbers of animals, pristine country and fairly low hunter pressure—is becoming harder and harder to come by.

Enter the special draw hunts.

Special-Draw Hunts: What Are They?

Virtually every state in the West offers several special hunts in which tag numbers are reduced, their issuance is tightly controlled and the game is managed for relatively high buck-to-doe or bull-to-cow ratios. Often, but not always, these hunts restrict hunters to the harvest of only old, mature bucks and bulls. Or, conversely, some special hunts are the only way to harvest a good cow elk for your freezer.

In many cases, special-draw hunts place weapons restrictions on hunters, limiting them to using a muzzleloader or archery tackle. And like just about every too-good-to-be-true deal in this world, it pays to read the fine print. For example, in the case of the best special hunts, competition for available tags is fierce. For example, the odds of drawing a tag in most of the areas I apply for each year are no better than 3 to 1—and they're usually much worse.

These difficult odds keep many people from applying. That's fine with me, but I still don't understand their thinking. Applying for these tags is a no-lose situation.

How to Apply for Special-Draw Hunts

The process begins in winter by contacting the game department of the state or states you're thinking about hunting. Ask for their upcoming year's hunting regulations, special-draw hunt application forms and any booklets required to apply for the special hunts. Don't dawdle; applications for some states are due as early as February. Fill them out and get them in on time with exactly the required amount of money. Remember to follow the rules regarding sending personal checks; some states require cashier's checks or money orders. If you draw, you receive the license and tag in the mail and away you go. If you don't draw, the state refunds all application fees except for a small processing fee.

Here's the kicker: In some cases, those who apply and do not draw a tag are given a "preference point" by the state. Preference points give preferential treatment in the drawings to those hunters who have applied for a certain type of hunt in previous years and not drawn a tag. In some cases you actually have to apply for several years before you're really in the game, thanks to the fact that there are more people with the maximum allowable number of preference points in the draw each year than there are tags available.

How Can You Lose?

You can't lose. If you draw, you're off on a terrific hunting adventure. If you don't, you get your money back and you can go ahead and hunt where you normally would anyway. Or, you've generated a preference point that will take you one step closer to drawing a tag on your dream hunt in the future. If the system confuses you, call United States Outfitters (USO) at (800) 845-9929, or employ a different professional licensing service to help you out. George Taulman's USO program is inexpensive and foolproof for the client and the best way I know of for the unattached hunter who doesn't have the time needed to keep up with what's happening with both special tag draws and hunting prospects in a number of states to get in the game. I've used the USO service extensively and have been very satisfied.

Maximum Quality, Minimal Cost

Maximum quality at minimum cost. That's what special-draw hunts are all about. The odds are long on drawing some of the more coveted permits. But someone has to draw and it might as well be you. However, you can't draw the tag if you don't play the game. For those serious about their elk hunting, the West's special-draw hunts are the best game in town.

How to Book a Guided Hunt

I've been on about two dozen guided elk hunts over the past three decades. The majority have been excellent. Unfortunately, some have not. The question is, how can you assure that your once-in-a-lifetime hunt will be a dream come true and not your worst nightmare?

Every year I meet excited hunters who book with the first elk outfitter they meet, simply because they don't want to go through the trouble of researching their trip. Some have a great hunt, but many do not. Quite honestly, there are a number of outfitters out there who are slicker than a snake oil salesman, fudging the facts just enough to get into your wallet. These guys show you lots of pictures of big bulls, giving you the impression that such success is

routine—but they don't tell you that the last time they killed one like that, Nixon was president, bell bottoms were hip and gas cost 30 cents a gallon. Frankly, people who don't do their homework and book a hunt with these guys get what they deserve.

Have realistic expectations about a guided hunting trip. First and foremost, booking a guided trip does not guarantee you'll harvest an animal. What it should guarantee is that you'll be provided with solid food, a comfortable camp, a guide who knows his stuff and is willing to work hard, equipment in good repair and the opportunity to hunt an area where you have a reasonably good chance of finding the animal you desire. Before contacting prospective outfitters, honestly answer the following questions about why you want to go hunting.

Which animal do you really want to hunt? Sounds basic, but many people do not target a single species as their priority. If hunting elk is your number-one goal, with mule deer and black bear secondary but nice if they happen along, you want to choose an outfitter in an area with lots of elk, not one in an area with lots of mulies or bears but only a few elk.

Is taking an animal more important than the quality of the experience? If so, you're setting yourself up for disappointment. Even the best guides and outfitters have weeks where the animals or weather don't cooperate. If an outfitter historically has gotten 75 percent of his clients an animal, you just may be the 25 percent that year who return empty-handed. There are no guarantees of success in fair-chase hunting. The best you can do is play the odds—and there are places where the chances for success are better than others.

Are you willing to do what it takes to prepare for the hunt? You can't expect to take an elk on a tough backpack hunt if you are not in good enough physical condition to make it up and down the mountain. Will you take time before the hunt to practice with your weapon, so that when your one good opportunity during a week's hunt presents itself, you are able to take advantage of it? The inability to walk and shoot are the two most common complaints outfitters have about clients.

What type of camp and hunting style will you be happy with? Is camping in a small backpack tent okay with you, or do you prefer the comfort of a lodge with a soft bed? Would you prefer to hunt from a pickup truck or hike among the peaks? Do you mind riding horses? Be honest with yourself or you'll end up being miserable.

Only after honestly answering these questions is it time to seek out individual outfitters. There are several ways to do this. I've met lots of top outfitters at some of the major hunting and fishing shows held around the country. Sport shows are a great place to interact personally with outfitters and get many of your questions answered on the spot. Advertisements in the back of magazines are another source. Using a booking agent who represents several different outfitters is one way to help shorten the research process. Word of mouth from friends who've hunted with a particular outfit before is perhaps your best source of information.

Always, *always* seek out and talk to references, people who have hunted elk with the outfitter before. Make sure that what you hear fits with your hunting attitudes and goals.

Give yourself enough time

Finally, give yourself enough time to plan your trip, locate a suitable outfitter and set aside vacation time. Most top outfitters book the majority of their hunts a year or more in advance. Rushing the process is a good way to make a mistake that could turn your dream into endless grief.

Ten Questions You Must Ask Prospective Outfitters

Before any money changes hands, ask prospective outfitters the following 10 questions.

1) ***What animals do you hunt?*** What are the species with top trophy potential in your area? If you want a big elk, with an average mule deer as your secondary goal, but the area has only mediocre elk and a few big mulies, you're probably hunting in the wrong place.

2) ***How many actual hunting days will I have?*** On a 10-day hunt, you may have 1 day travel time each way in and out of the hunting area, cutting the actual hunt time to 8 days. If you're stranded in base camp for extra days because the outfitter is having problems, will he allow you to extend your hunt to compensate for missed days afield that were not your fault? The outfitter can't control the weather, but he should be in control of his equipment, staff and scheduling.

3) ***How many hunters and support people will there be in camp?*** To avoid overcrowding, you want to know how many other hunters will be in hunting camp. Also ask if your guide doubles as the cook, horse wrangler and wood cutter. Generally, it's better if the guide does nothing except take you hunting; it's better to have his energy expended in the field!

4) ***How many hunters are there per guide?*** Do you have the guide all to yourself or will you be sharing him with another client? Though it costs more, it's almost always more productive to hunt one-on-one. If you get to camp and your booked one-on-one hunt is suddenly a two-on-one affair, immediately solve the problem with the outfitter.

5) ***How long have you been hunting in your area?*** How long have your guides worked for you? I prefer to hunt with people who have been outfitting an area for at least three seasons and who, therefore, know the area and area game movements well. Also, the outfitter will rarely be taking you hunting himself. You want a guide with experience hunting both the species and area you're targeting. *Don't settle for a first-year guide as your primary guide.*

6) ***Bowhunters: Are your guides experienced bowhunters themselves?*** Have they successfully guided bowhunters before? It's important for bowhunters to have a guide who understands the unique requirements and challenges of hunting with archery tackle.

7) ***What percentage of your clients are repeat customers?*** If the outfitter was lousy and there was no game in the area, he'd probably not have many repeat clients. Repeat business is one indicator of a reputable outfit.

8) ***What does the hunt package cost?*** You'll be quoted a hunt cost of, say, $4000 for a horseback wilderness elk hunt. Now ask about any "hidden" costs like licenses and tags (rarely included in the hunt price), trophy and meat care, tips and gratuities, additional charges if you take another animal, and so on. Is there a "trophy fee" for actually harvesting an animal or for taking an animal that scores exceptionally well by record book standards? These "extras" can add hundreds of dollars to a hunt's base price. No one likes to be surprised.

Ten Questions continued ...

9) ***Do you have references I can contact?*** Ask not only for a list of successful clients but also for clients who did not get game on their hunt. Ask for references within the last three years. Spend a few bucks, call them all and ask lots of questions regarding all aspects of the hunt. If an outfitter won't provide references, avoid him like the plague.

10) ***Do you have a written hunt contract?*** Years ago, a handshake and deposit were enough. Today they're not. Make sure the outfitter has a prepared hunt agreement that spells everything out in writing, including hunt cost, duration, species to be hunted, guide-to-hunter ratio, specific hunt dates, his cancellation policy, etc. Make sure he has liability insurance. Check with the state to make sure he is licensed and bonded. (In some states, notably Wyoming, it is against the law to hire an outfitter who is not registered and licensed.) Before signing the contract, have all your questions answered. Outfitters that don't have the time to spend with you on these matters are more interested in your money than your satisfaction; hunt with someone else.

For More Information

In addition to writing or calling individual game departments, you can also glean information from various states' internet Web sites. They can be found at http://www.state.or.us (the "or" is for Oregon; substitute the two-letter abbreviation of the state you're interested in here). Here are addresses and phone numbers for relevant state game departments:

Alaska Department of Fish & Game
P.O. Box 25526
Juneau, AK 99802
(907) 465-4190

Arizona Game & Fish Department
2222 W. Greenway Rd.
Phoenix, AZ 85023
(602) 942-3000

California Department of Fish & Game
3211 S St.
Sacramento, CA 95816
(916) 227-2271

Colorado Division of Wildlife
6060 Broadway
Denver, CO 80216
(303) 297-1192

Idaho Fish & Game Department
600 S. Walnut
P.O. Box 25
Boise, ID 83707
(208) 334-3700

Montana Department of Fish, Wildlife & Parks
P.O. Box 200701
Helena, MT 59620
(406) 444-2535

Nevada Department of Wildlife

P.O. Box 10678
Reno, NV 89520
(702) 688-1500

New Mexico Game & Fish Department

P.O. Box 25112
Santa Fe, NM 87504
(505) 827-7911

Oregon Department of Fish & Wildlife

P.O. Box 59
Portland, OR 97207
(503) 872-5268

Utah Division of Wildlife Resources

1596 W. North Temple
Salt Lake City, UT 84114
(801) 538-4700

Washington Department of Fish & Wildlife

600 Capitol Way N.
Olympia, WA 98501
(360) 902-2200

Wyoming Game & Fish Department

5400 Bishop Blvd.
Cheyenne, WY 82206
(307) 777-4600

Topographic Maps

Topographic maps can often be obtained from backpacking stores and some larger hunting shops throughout the West. Maps can also be ordered from the U.S. Geological Survey, Distribution Branch, Federal Center, Denver, CO 80225; phone (303) 236-5900. First call and ask for a state order map, off of which specific individual maps can be ordered. The people here are very nice and will help you get what you need.

National Forests

These regional headquarters of the U.S. Forest Service can provide a complete list of national forests within their region. From these regional forest headquarters offices you can obtain current information on logging operations or fires as well as purchase specific national forest maps. The U.S. Forest Service and its regional offices nationwide can also be found on the World Wide Web at www.fs.fed.us.

Region 1 (Montana, northern Idaho):
(406) 329-3089; 329-2411 fax

Region 2 (Colorado, part of Wyoming):
(303) 275-5350; 275-5366 fax

Region 3 (Arizona, New Mexico):
(505) 842-3076; 476-3300 fax

Region 4 (Nevada, southern Idaho, western Wyoming):
(801) 625-5262; 625-5240 fax

Region 5 (California):
(415) 705-1837; 705-1097 fax

Region 6 (Oregon, Washington):
(503) 808-2971; 326-5044 fax

Bureau of Land Management (BLM)

Information on current land status, logging operations and fires as well as maps of BLM lands are available from these regional offices. Each state's BLM Web site can be found at www.ak.blm.gov ("ak" is for Alaska; substitute the two-letter abbreviation of the state you're interested in here).

Alaska:	(907) 271-5960
Arizona:	(602) 417-9200
California:	(916) 978-4400
Colorado:	(303) 239-3600
Idaho:	(208) 373-3930
Montana:	(406) 255-2782
Nevada:	(702) 861-6400
New Mexico:	(505) 438-7400
Oregon/Washington:	(503) 952-6027
Utah:	(801) 539-4001
Washington:	(see Oregon)
Wyoming:	(307) 775-6256

State-by-State Elk Herd Estimates

The following herd estimates were provided by individual state and provincial game departments. Remember, these numbers are just that—estimates. We provide them here for general information only. Be sure to contact each individual state or province you're considering hunting before making any final plans. The total figure reflects free-ranging elk, which includes those found in national parks but not those found in pens or held on private, fenced enclosures.

State/Province	**Estimated Elk Population**
Alaska	1,500
Arizona	25,000
Arkansas	450
California	8,000
Colorado	220,000
Idaho	118,000
Kentucky	170
Michigan	1,000
Montana	100,000
Nevada	4,250
New Mexico	58,000
North Dakota	700
Oklahoma	800
Oregon	130,000
Pennsylvania	350
South Dakota	4,000
Texas	350
Utah	63,000
Washington	60,000
Wisconsin	50
Wyoming	110,000
Canada	
Alberta	26,000
British Columbia	43,000
Manitoba	8,500
Saskatchewan	12,000
Total elk:	**995,570**

Chapter 9

After Your Elk Is Down

I've seen it so many times that I've come to expect it. The hunter, bagging his first elk, is sky-high with emotion. All that hard work, planning, praying and hoping has paid off. The shot was a clean one and the elk went down quickly. Nothing could be better! After a round of high-fives and back-slaps, we walk over to him.

The hunter is still smiling, but you can see his brain turning. Man, he's thinking, these elk are big! As we try to roll the bull into position for some pictures, the mass and bulk of 700 pounds of dead weight becomes even more evident. The hunter is still as proud as he's ever been, but unless he's brain-dead, he's just beginning to realize that with elk, you don't simply field dress them and then drag the carcass back to the truck as you would a deer.

We have a big job ahead of us. For me, however, caring for an elk is a labor of love. After all, percentage-wise, few hunters have the opportunity each fall. Unfortunately, elk rarely go down on some nice flat, grassy piece of real estate near a road. There always seems to be a steep hill—or mountain—to contend with. Maybe it's just because I remember the tough ones more, but it always seems to be raining or snowing when I shoot an elk, which seems always to have expired a long way from camp. On the downhill side.

No matter. With the right tools and some sweat equity, the job goes quickly. Even packing meat, which can be very hard work indeed, doesn't seem so bad now with the pressure off. And later, when the family sits down to that first dinner of thick elk steaks, it's easy to forget how much work it really was. Heck, right about now I'm starting to think, it really wasn't all that tough. And you know, next year we ought to go hunt that far canyon we're always talking about. That's where the big bulls just have to be! Sure, getting them out will be tough, but we can do it. We proved it this year!

Selective memory. It's like that with elk hunters, who can't wait for next season, to do it one more time ...

Basic Field Dressing

On backpack hunts, you'll have to be ready, willing and able to butcher your elk, then pack hundreds of pounds of meat to the nearest road. Boning the meat is the smart thing to do here.

We've all heard the saying, "The fun's over when you pull the trigger!" That statement is never more true than with elk hunting.

Basically, elk hunting is hard work. But if you think it's been tough up till now, just wait until you shoot an elk in rough country, miles from the nearest road. Throw in some nasty weather, like a snowstorm or thunder and a little lightning. Stir in a pinch of thick brush and a steep mountain between you and civilization. For good measure, add a dash of slippery-as-snot trail—if there's any trail at all—and you begin to get the picture.

Getting your elk off the mountain to the butcher shop in prime condition is no easy task. Every year hunters lose meat to spoilage or the butcher's trim knife because they were not prepared to handle the task. Don't let this happen to you.

The Right Tools

Meat care begins with the right tools. For elk hunting, you're going to need at least one, but preferably two, hunting knives with strong blades so sharp they scare you. I like clip-point blades between 4 and 6 inches long, with handles made of either bone or a no-slip handle material like Zytel. You'll need a sharpening stone or steel, a lightweight saw or hatchet for splitting the brisket and cutting off the antlers, 50 feet of nylon parachute cord or thin-diameter rope and four or five elk-sized cotton meat sacks. Don't get the cheap cheesecloth bags; buy the ones that are heavy enough to be washed and reused. They're the only ones strong enough for this job.

Be sure to have at least one roll of fluorescent flagging or a GPS so you can mark the spot where the elk dropped in case you have to come back for subsequent trips. A headlamp is cheap at twice the price when you have to butcher an elk after dark.

Elk are big animals, requiring the right tools to take care of them in the field. These include a sharp hunting knife and sharpener, small saw for cutting off antlers and sawing through the brisket and pelvis, rubber gloves to prevent accidental infection, and quality game bags. A head lamp will make field dressing and butchering in the dark much easier than a standard flashlight.

Your goal is to prevent meat spoilage. You do that by cooling the meat, and doing it quickly, remembering that on big-bodied animals like elk, meat can spoil both from the inside and outside. You must also strive to keep the meat as clean as possible, free from dirt and its inherent bacteria.

Secure the Elk

Before any cutting begins, you have to secure the elk, which often has expired on a steep side-hill. That's where the cord or rope comes in: Use it to tie antlers or legs to a tree or bush to hold the animal in place as you work. Point the butt down-hill if you can. Butchering an elk is much easier with two people, so if you can get some help, I advise you to do so.

Field Dress or Quarter?

There are two ways to clean any big-game animal, including elk. You can do the basic field-dressing routine, which means first gutting the animal. Or you can take the quarters, backstrap and neck off without gutting. I do either, depending on the circumstances.

Field Dressing. The basic field-dressing procedure is the same as it is with deer and other big game (except on a larger scale), so I won't detail it here. You remove the innards, including the anus, taking care not to puncture the bladder or stomach; as with any field dressing, you want to do everything possible to keep these contents off the meat. Make sure you remove the heart, lungs and entire esophagus.

I field dress an elk when I am not going to be able to finish the job right away, like when I might have to leave the carcass to cool overnight before packing it out. When I do this, I lay the animal on its back, then cut the front shoulders so they lie out away from the carcass and cut the hams to the ball joint so they, too, are opened up enough to cool down.

Quartering without Dressing. These days I prefer simply to quarter the animal without exposing its guts. This is a less messy and smelly process, and you don't lose any meat.

To do that, roll the elk onto one side and use your knife to remove the hindquarter through the ball joint and the front shoulder by cutting

Quartering an Elk without Field Dressing

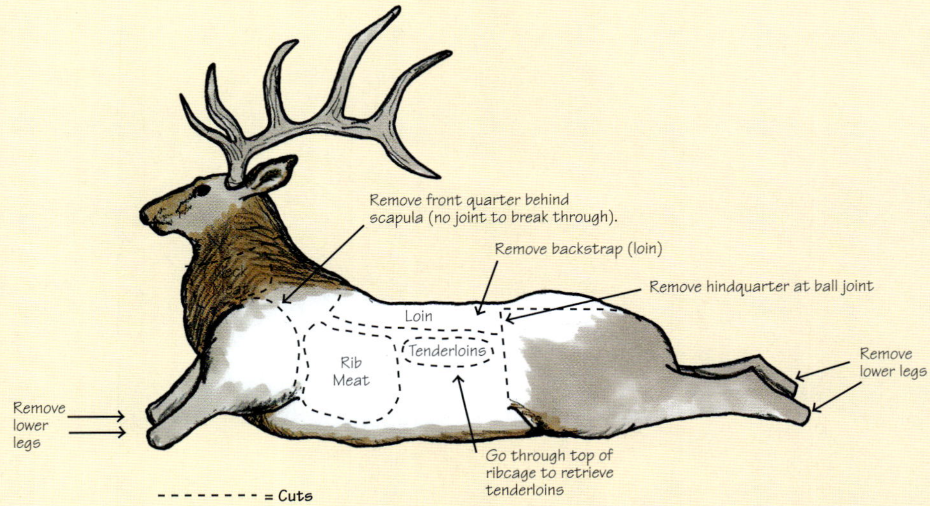

Yes, you can get the meat off an elk—and cooled quickly—without field dressing the animal. Here are the cuts to make.

behind the scapula, leaving the hide on until the quarter is either hung or ready for boning and insertion into the meat sacks. That helps keep dirt off the meat itself. Next, remove the backstrap, half of the neck meat and the meat off the outside of the rib cage; or if you like, use your saw to cut the ribs completely off. (I rarely do this, though.) You then roll the elk over and repeat. To get the tenderloins out—they're located inside the carcass on each side of the backbone—use the lightweight saw to cut through the top of the rib cage. When ready for bagging, skin the quarters out. Voilà! One butchered elk, without the big mess of field dressing it first.

I virtually always bone out my elk meat for two reasons. One, it gets rid of excess weight that I would otherwise have to pack down the mountain. And two, removing the bone opens the meat up and facilitates cooling. Thick chunks of elk meat, like those found on the hams and neck, will spoil quickly near the bone unless they are cooled properly. Boning helps this process. Hunters with the luxury of packhorses often like to keep the bone in, as it can make loading quarters into pack boxes easier.

Some hunters like to take the liver, heart and tongue, all of which make some fine eating. An elk liver is about the size of a football, and a heart about the size of an elongated softball, so you'll have plenty of extra packing if you want them. I often do.

Dreams Do Come True ... But Don't Count on It!

Let me tell you about a fantasy that actually came true on the 21st bull elk I took. After years of packing meat either on my back or atop packhorses, I was invited to hunt a private New Mexico ranch. The nice 6x6 I shot was a big-bodied critter, but it didn't matter. The guide drove the truck right up to him, winched him into the bed—whole—and drove back to the barn, where the elk was hung and his innards removed. The butchering took place indoors in a clean, sterile environment.

Now that's heaven on earth! But don't count on it. On an on-your-own elk hunt, you're going to have to handle the butchering and packing chores yourself. And while it's hard work, I look upon it as a labor of love. It means both that I've been successful and that my family can look forward to a year's worth of some of the most delicious and nutritious meat in all the world.

Meat Care

When you shoot a mature elk, there's a lot of meat to care for. Long-time Montana outfitter Merritt Pride uses his ranch scales to weigh the meat from most of the bulls his clients shoot. The average age of the bulls is 3½ years, and the average weight of the meat (with the bone in) is between 330 and 430 pounds. That's much larger than pratically any deer on the hoof!

Elk have thick muscles, which means that even in cold weather, cooling the meat can be a problem. This is especially true near the hip sockets and shoulder joints and around the neck. Elk also have thick hides, which can impede cooling. While some hunters like to leave the hide on to help keep the meat clean, any elk shot when day-time temperatures reach about 70° F during the day with no frost at night—almost all rut hunts fall into this category—need to be skinned immediately to facilitate cooling as well. When skinning in the field to get the meat cooled off, leave the fat in place. This protects the meat from flies and dirt and will reduce the amount of trim you have when it's time to cut and wrap your elk. You can either trim it off just before packing it down the hill or when you reach the butchering location. On late-season hunts, when temperatures drop to or below freezing, the hide can safely be left on, as long as the body cavity has been opened up or the elk quartered.

Nutritional Comparison

According to the U.S. Department of Agriculture, here's how a 3-ounce cooked portion of elk meat compares with other meats in the nutrition department.

Meat	Calories	Fat (grams)	Cholesterol (milligrams)	Protein (grams)
Elk, leg cut	135	1	67	24
Venison, leg cut	139	5	62	22
Beef round steak	189	8	81	27
Beef tenderloin	174	8	72	24
Beef brisket	223	13	77	24
Ground beef (72% lean)	248	18	77	20
Ground beef (82% lean)	213	12	84	25
Lamb leg roast	153	6	74	24
Lamb loin chop	183	8	80	25
Veal cutlet	155	4	112	28
Pork shoulder	207	13	82	22
Pork loin, top	219	13	80	24
Chicken breast, with skin	167	7	72	25
Chicken breast, without skin	140	3	72	24
Turkey, dark meat	159	6	72	24
Turkey, white meat	133	3	59	26
Bass, broiled	167	3	62	18
Salmon, broiled	140	5	60	21
Halibut, steamed	111	3	62	20

Should You Wash the Meat?

An old wives' tale says never to put water on meat in the field. I've found that as long as you dry the meat or carcass thoroughly after washing it, rinsing off blood and any intestinal juices enhances the flavor of your meat. Also, in extremely hot weather, cooling can be facilitated by washing meat off in a cold mountain stream. And at home, soaking bloody meat in a saltwater solution will leech out even the most stubborn blood and body juices. Just make sure the meat is dried out before you wrap it for the freezer.

Once the meat has been washed and dried, take pains to keep it dry. Moist meat is a haven for bacteria growth; so even in the field, keep your meat under cover when it rains or snows.

The Right Game Bags

Use only heavy-duty cloth game bags, assuming they are breathable. The cheapest cheesecloth game bags will rip and tear, each hole an engraved invitation for flies and other bugs. The heavier game bags will keep the bugs out and help prevent dirt from getting in.

Many people advise never to use plastic bags for meat care. I use them all the time. They keep my backpack bag from getting all bloody and smelling like an elk. However, once I get back to camp, I take the meat out of the plastic bags and put it into cheesecloth game bags before hanging it to air out and cool down. If you use plastic bags, buy only super-heavy bags. Trash compactor bags are much heavier than even the thickest lawn care bags and are very difficult to puncture or rip. No matter what kind of bags you use, ensure that they are not chemically treated.

Ice It Down

You've worked too hard bagging an elk and then packing the meat to the trailhead. Why would you forget about it on the drive home? Many elk hunters do, though, then wonder why that bull they shot tastes so "gamey." It's not the elk—it's the way they transported their meat.

If you are traveling hundreds of miles home from your elk hunt by vehicle, be sure to bring along two or three large ice chests to transport your meat home. I bone out my meat, cool it down, place it in plastic trash compactor bags, then ice it generously for the long drive. If you just throw it in the back of the truck and don't keep it iced, you're asking for tainted flavor at best and spoilage at worst.

The keys to meat care are simple: Cool it down.; keep it clean; keep the bugs and dirt off. If it gets wet or you wash it in water, get it dry and keep it dry. Ice it down in a clean ice chest for the drive home. Taking your time to do it all right while in the field, then transporting it properly, will ensure that your family will be dining on what many consider to be the finest wild meat in the Lower 48.

Trophy Care

If you plan on having your elk mounted, you'll need to cape the head rather than randomly skin the animal. Some hunters like to save capes anyway, selling them to their local taxidermist. Regardless, you need to know the basic fundamentals of caping to get the job done.

Caping Elk Heads

Before starting, remember that you need to leave lots of hide for the taxidermist to work with. Make the first cut from the belly line approximately 3 feet behind the front shoulder, tracing a line parallel to the front leg and stopping on the backbone. Now follow straight along the backbone up to about the middle of the ears. From here, make a 45-degree diagonal cut to the base of each antler, which results in a Y-shaped cut in the back of the head. Next, skin out the front portion of the elk, including the neck to the base of the skull, taking care not to puncture the hide but trying to remove all meat and fat. When done, roll the elk over and do the other side. When finished, you can remove the head by using your knife to cut through the Atlas joint, which is where the head swivels on the top of the neck. You don't need a saw or hatchet for this; your knife is enough.

Caping an Elk

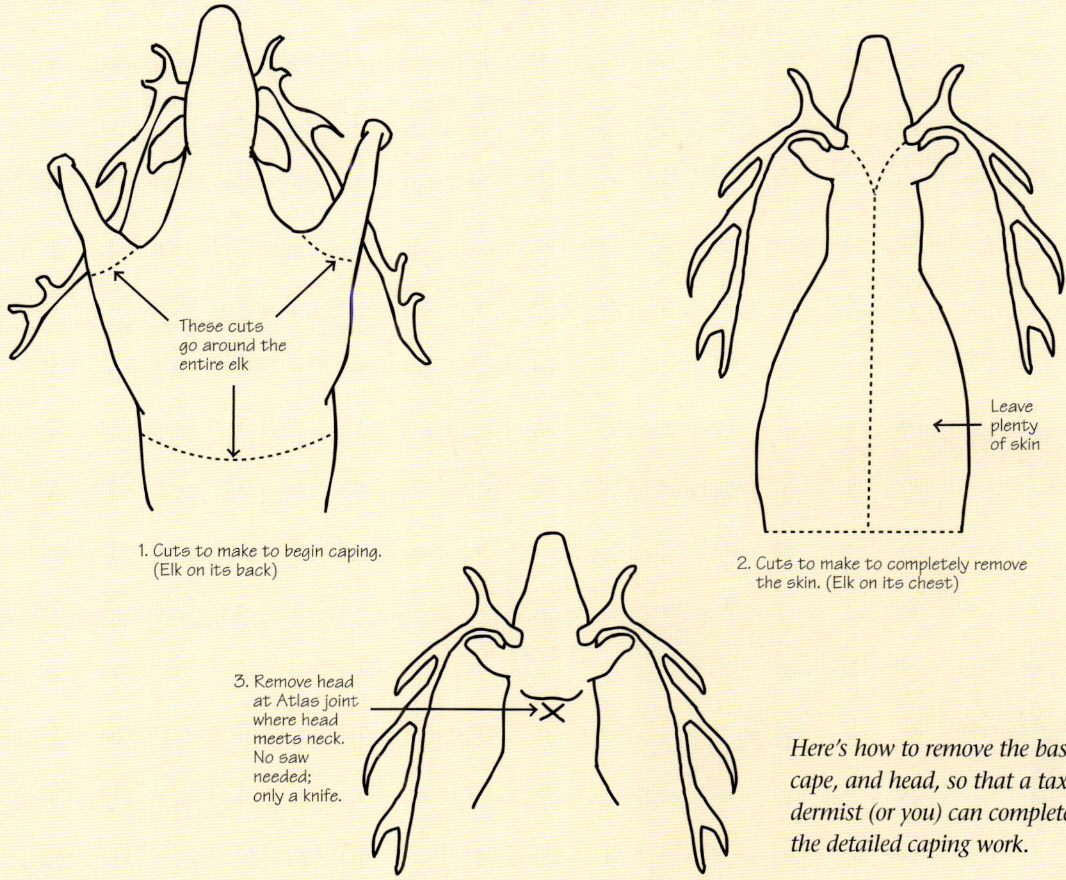

Here's how to remove the basic cape, and head, so that a taxidermist (or you) can complete the detailed caping work.

When possible—when there are packhorses or if I can lug the head to the truck—I like to leave the skin on the head and pay my taxidermist to do the rest. They're professionals and for a little money will do it right. However, if you're going to be afield for more than a day, it's best if you cape the head out yourself.

To do this, first cut the ears loose from the head, cutting as close to the skull as possible. Next, work the hide off around the antler bases. It's tight here, and while you can do it with your knife if you're careful, a blunt object like a screwdriver will make it easy to pry the hide off cleanly. When you reach the eyes, take care not to cut the eyelids. I slide a finger into the eye socket and lift the lid out, which helps avoid tearing. Continue working down the face, leaving a thick piece of cartilage on the skin at the nose, making sure to cut the lips off well back inside the mouth.

If you're going to be in camp for any length of time, especially in hot weather, you'll need to turn the ears inside out and split the lips. Ears are done by carefully skinning down into the ear itself, pushing from the underside with a blunt stick. Once you get them started you can sometimes use your finger or a blunt, flat stick to work down into the ear and separate the cartilage from the skin. Splitting lips involves painstakingly slicing them open to promote cooling. It's a sort of delicate operation, so take your time and be careful. Visiting your local taxidermist before going hunting and having him or her show you the basics of these two procedures is a good idea.

Once the cape is removed, hang it in a cool, shady place so air can circulate around it and cool it down quickly. Keep it out of the sun. In cool weather, you should be able to keep it this way for

Elk Ivories?

Novice elk hunters often overlook the "ivories," a nickname given to the two canine teeth found in an elk's upper jaw. Ivories were highly prized by both native tribes and mountain men, who wore them as pendants and used them to decorate garments, necklaces and shields. Be sure to save your elk ivories; they're a unique trophy and one you'll certainly treasure forever.

Antler Care

In the field, caring for antlers is simple. All you have to do is cut off the top of the skull using your saw or hatchet (see diagram). To know where to cut, draw an imaginary line through the bottom third of the eye sockets parallel to the base of the antlers, and start sawing. Once this has been cut off, take a little time to remove any brain and eye matter, and cut away the biggest chunks of meat. Also remember that it is always easier to remove the antlers after the head has been skinned back.

Some hunters like a "European" mount, so called because it the common way European hunters display their trophies. The Europeans simply skin the head out, then remove the lower jaw, keeping the top half of the skull attached. In the field, you'll again need to remove brain and eye matter, as well as excess meat. European mounts are a handsome way to show off your elk antlers if a full head mount is not desired.

Take your time in all phases of trophy field care. Remember the old carpenter's adage—measure twice, cut once—to avoid accidentally cutting a big hole in the cape or, heaven forbid, your own fingers. The result will be a handsome reminder of one of the most exciting and memorable hunting adventures of your life!

several days without worry. However, if you're going to be in the backcountry for a long time, you'll have to salt the cape to prevent it from spoiling and having the hair fall out during the tanning process. Don't salt the cape without turning the ears, or they will dry so hard that they will not be flexible enough to be turned later! It takes about five to seven pounds of salt to salt an elk cape adequately. Make sure you diligently work the salt into the cape with your fingers, taking pains to get enough in the ear, eye, nose and lip areas. Using a pair of rubber gloves will help prevent salt from getting into all those little nicks and cuts you've gotten on your fingers and hands during the week. Once the hide has been salted, roll it up fur-side-out and store it out of the sun.

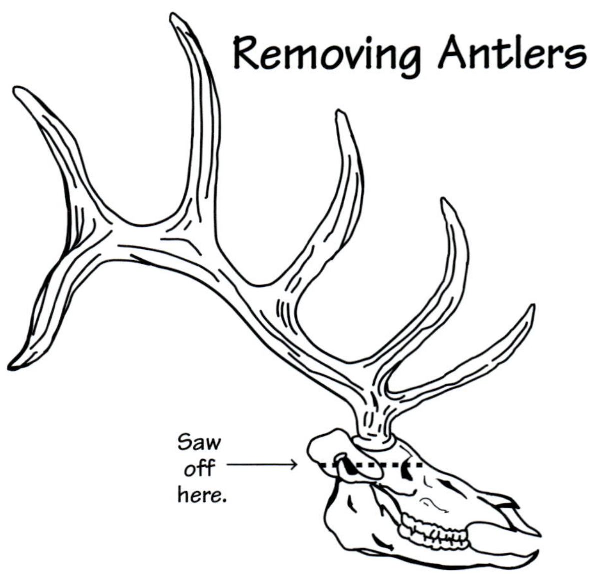

Chapter 10

The Future of Elk Hunting

This may be hard to believe for those who never hunted elk back in the 1960s and 1970s: Back then, finding an elk to shoot was not all that easy. Elk numbers were growing, but for those of us who were fanatical Rocky Mountain big-game hunters, the emphasis was on mule deer, of which there were plenty.

As we approach the millennium, all that has changed. Today it is the mule deer that is being pushed out of its range by the proliferation of elk. Here's how that happened.

At the turn of the century, Western mountain ranges were almost solidly covered with old-growth forests. Settlers coming West could not envision a shortage of firewood and lumber. These forests were heaven-on-earth for loggers but mediocre habitat for supporting large numbers of big game, whose numbers were far greater in the foothills and on the prairies.

During the first decade of the 20th century, several large wildfires raged through these virgin forests. In 1910, a tornado of fire swept through the northern Rocky Mountains; when it was through, an area that had been a giant forest was reduced to a blackened landscape—much like large areas of Yellowstone National Park following the fires of the late 1980s. These burned areas became lush meadows of nutritious grasses and forbs within a few years. In little more than a decade, elk, deer and bears moved in. Game populations began to soar ...

While state records from the turn of the century are hard to come by, they tell us that about 3,000 elk were harvested in the year 1900. In 20 years, that number had increased to around 20,000. The total Western states' elk harvest peaked at about 140,000 animals in the 1960s.

However, immediately following the peak harvest years of the 1960s, the top elk-producing states began experiencing a slow decline in the overall elk harvest, a reflection in the decline in overall elk numbers. Why? Three reasons stand out. First, the lush habitat created by fire 50 years earlier had begun returning to old-growth forests—habitat not suited to maximum ungulate production. Second, elk hunting regulations during those "heyday" years were much more liberal than they are today. Almost all states had rifle seasons open during the September rut, and seasons often stayed open until December, when snows pushed elk out of the high country down into more easily accessible winter ranges. And third, the wheel of man's progress continued to turn, slowly encroaching into prime elk habitat with: new towns and cities; mining; dirt roads that made backcountry access easier for hunters; and increased cattle and sheep grazing on public forest lands. All contributed to the decline of habitat quality and thus a reduction in elk numbers.

Fire can remove security cover, but the burned-over areas will soon produce lots of nutritious forage.

Fortunately, state game departments and hunters recognized the need for improved elk management programs that included controlled burns and overall habitat management, more careful management of elk hunting seasons, and a beginning of balance between the needs of the timber industry and wildlife habitat. Taken together, the result has been an explosion in elk herds across the West.

Thanks to transplants, elk have returned to many states east of the Mississippi River for the first time in centuries. States like Wisconsin and Kentucky have few elk today, but both states anticipate limited elk seasons in a few years. Minnesota annually issues a few tags. Michigan has been issuing between 300 and 400 permits a year in recent years. Further west, who'd ever have thought that states like Texas, Oklahoma and the Dakotas would become elk-hunting states? They have, and while tags are very limited, the hunting is excellent.

However, that doesn't mean there are not problems that need to be solved in terms of elk management today. There are. Here are some of them.

Backcountry Roads. The largest impact logging operations have on the long-term health of an elk herd is not the cutting of trees but the building of roads that open formerly wild, inaccessible areas to an influx of elk hunters. To combat the problem, many states are closing or restricting access to these roads during elk hunting seasons.

Security Cover Loss. When habitat is modified without concern for both game and nongame species—by logging or construction of housing and recreational developments like ski resorts—animals lose. For example, it has been shown that elk require fingers of thick cover in which to travel from place to place. Without this cover, they either refuse to make the trip or are so vulnerable to hunters that they can easily be overharvested. Developments that do not consider

Despite the resurgence of elk across North America, state game biologists continue to face the challenges a growing human population places on our ever-shrinking wildlife habitat.

their impact on summer/winter range migration corridors can destroy an elk herd.

Ranchers vs. Elk. One of the growing concerns in many Western states is the plundering of ranchers' crops by rapidly growing elk herds. In many areas, elk descend on crops like overgrown locusts in winter, eating everything in sight. Who can blame them? They're just trying to fill their bellies. But many ranchers, naturally, don't take kindly to this and want every elk in the valley killed. Yet hunting access can be a problem. States continue to try to balance all these needs—between landowners, hunters and elk herds. It's a tough job.

Predators. With states rapidly enacting legislation (usually by the initiative process and not at the recommendation of game departments) that protects large predators, elk herds continue to fall prey to these hungry animals. The elimination of the trapping and poisoning of coyotes and the elimination of the use of hounds in hunting mountain lions has resulted in dramatic drops in elk calf numbers in some areas. The reintroduction of the wolf to Yellowstone National Park and other federal lands throughout the West will certainly result in increased elk predation. Every elk a predator kills is an elk a hunter does not have an opportunity to put in his own freezer. These increased predator numbers will have a huge impact on Western mule deer herds, too. Once again, balancing the needs of the elk, habitat, predators and human hunters is a very tough job.

Elk Herd Composition. State game managers can closely control a specific elk herd's makeup—specifically, the bull-to-cow ratio and the number of older, mature bulls in that herd. These same managers have begun to survey hunters and the general public about what they want to see in their state's elk herds. Some hunters prefer lots of elk and the chance to harvest any bull or cow for their freezers. Others want a chance to shoot a trophy bull. Many states try to do both: have open areas where elk numbers remain high but where harvest levels reduce the chances of any bull living long

Balancing predators with elk management is a tough proposition for biologists these days. Booming mountain lion numbers throughout the West have resulted in reduced numbers of elk calves in some areas.

There are more elk in North America today than at any time since the turn of the century. This incredible wildlife success story is due largely to the effort of America's sportsmen, who have poured millions of dollars and countless hours of habitat improvement work into elk country.

enough to achieve trophy status; and have limited-entry areas, where harvests are closely monitored to permit many bulls to reach old age. Some states have imposed antler point restrictions to address the issue too. To be a part of this process, elk hunters must continue to make their desires known to game departments.

The Anti-Hunting Movement. I've spent a lot of time in the trenches fighting anti-hunters over the years. I've learned several things about them. One, many are fanatical about their cause. For them there will never be any compromise, no middle ground. Another is that many of the officers of anti-hunting groups are in it for the fat salaries and perks they receive annually. They're nothing more than mercenaries, hired guns fighting as much for themselves as for any cause. Also, many refuse to acknowledge the real way nature works, and they don't want to know anything about the cruel way it kills. Finally, these groups have no shame. Some will even lie, cheat or commit criminal acts in the name of their "cause."

The anti-hunters will not go away ... ever. All hunters must be willing to spend time and money fighting them on both the local and national level. Your beliefs, needs, wants and concerns—to have wild places to hunt and then to be able to do the hunting—are important. Do not let these groups win.

Get involved in the fight with your voice, your time, your dollars and your votes. Write letters to newspapers, congressional representatives and the governor's office. If your children are being taught an anti-hunting agenda in school (and don't think it isn't happening across the country, because it is, more than you might think), voice your concerns emphatically. Support pro-hunting organizations that support you and your beliefs.

The Rocky Mountain Elk Foundation

One of the biggest boosts ever for the future of elk and elk hunting was the creation of the Rocky Mountain Elk Foundation (RMEF) in 1984. The dream of a handful of average, everyday elk hunters, RMEF has grown into one of the nation's largest conservation organizations with chapters in all 50 states and around the world. The organization has raised untold millions of dollars to preserve and enhance elk habitat. RMEF works closely with state game departments on all types of projects involving elk and has brought together often-feuding factions like hunters, ranchers, governmental agencies and others in a never-ending quest to improve the elk's situation in North America. It publishes both *Bugle*, a bimonthly magazine, and *Wild Outdoor World*, a bimonthly children's conservation education magazine.

For more information about becoming an RMEF member, contact the group at P.O. Box 8249, 2291 W. Broadway, Missoula, MT 59807. You can e-mail RMEF at rmef@rmef.org or call the office by dialing 1-800-CALL ELK.

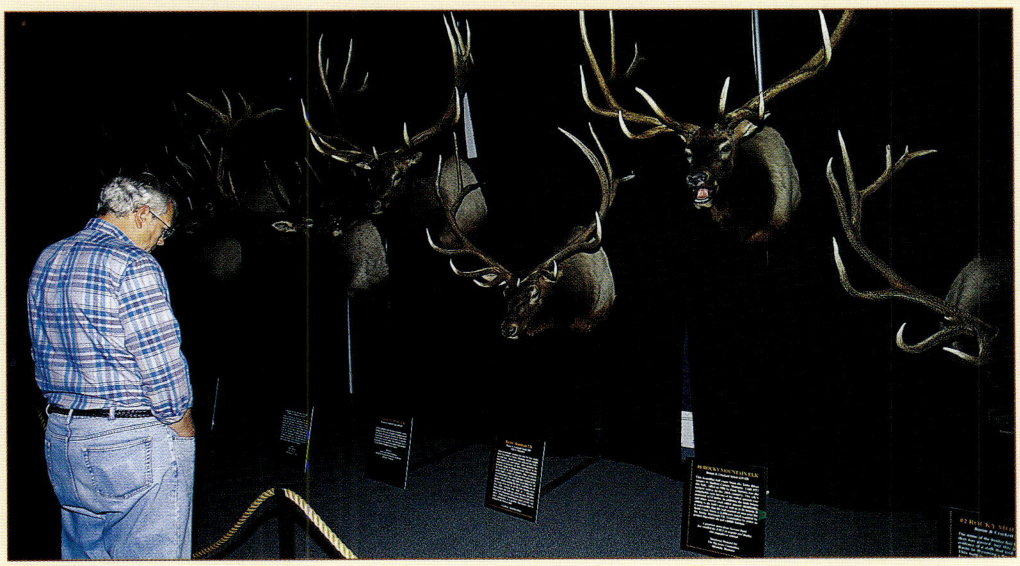

The future of elk hunting—and of all sport hunting—lies in our ability to recruit new hunters into the fold, including women and children. In addition, all outdoorsmen and women must be ready, willing and able to do battle with the ever-present anti-hunting movement.

Unless we all become involved in the fight against the anti-hunting movement and sway the majority of Americans who are noncommittal on the issue of sport hunting, we will continually stand on the brink of defeat.

The future of elk hunting is indeed a bright one. But like anything worth having, it doesn't come easily or cheaply. All of us who love elk—and elk hunting—need to become involved in the process. In so doing, we will ensure that there will continue to be elk, elk hunting and the magnificent country that elk call home for our children's children to enjoy.

INDEX